HARLEY-DAVIDSON
SHOVELHEAD

Tom Murphy

Motorbooks International
Publishers & Wholesalers ®

First published in 1996 by Motorbooks International Publishers & Wholesalers, 729 Prospect Avenue, PO Box 1, Osceola, WI 54020 USA

Motorbooks International books are also available at discounts in bulk quantity for industrial or sales-promotional use. For details write to Special Sales Manager at the Publisher's address

Library of Congress Cataloging-in-Publication Data
Murphy, Tom
 Harley-Davidson shovelhead motorcycles/Tom Murphy.
   p. cm. —(Motorbooks International motorcycle color history)
 Includes index.
 ISBN 0-7603-0164-6 (pbk.: alk. paper)
 1. Harley-Davidson motorcycle. I. Title. II. Series.
TL448.H3M874 1996
629.227'5—dc20   96-10200

On the front cover: This 1969 FLH Electra Glide was the last year for the "generator" motor. The "cone" motor appeared late in 1969. *Jeff Hackett*

On the frontispiece: A factory shot of the original Shovelhead engine, which was introduced in 1966 and available until 1984. *Harley-Davidson*

On the title page: This 75th Anniversary Edition 1200cc Electra Glide was built in 1978 to commemorate 75 years of the Harley-Davidson Motor Company. *Harley-Davidson*

On the back cover: (Top) This 1971 FLH is as stock as they come. *Jeff Hackett* (Bottom) The 1971 Super Glide sported an unusually styled (that's putting it kindly) fiberglass rear fender.

Printed in Hong Kong

Contents

Acknowledgments

Without the help of all the Shovelhead riders out there, this book wouldn't have been possible. So many people I met only over the telephone went out of their way to help me that I think their names should be listed as co-authors, if it were possible.

Primarily, thanks to Harley-Davidson, in the persona of Dr. Martin Jack Rosenblum, historian and chief guardian of the faith for H-D and Steve Piehl, H-D's Manager of Public Relations, both of whom spent considerable time insuring I had much-needed aid and assistance when it came to accuracy in this manuscript. Also I owe a lot to my shepherd, Greg Field, who kept me on the proper path through all this, and to my editor, Lee (we need more information) Klancher, without whom, I'd still be writing short stories.

To everybody who stood still while I asked for "one more shot," or sent valuable pictures to a voice on the other end of a telephone line, thank you—it's your bikes that made this book. The only parts I accomplished all by myself are the mistakes.

—Tom Murphy
Campbell, California

Introduction

Every Harley owner seems to have his or her individual preference when it comes to a specific year and model of Harley-Davidson. Some of us lean toward the new bikes, figuring the Evo is the best thing to happen to the V-twin since American Machine and Foundry (AMF) went away. Others think H-D quit building motorcycle engines when the valves moved up into the head. My preference has always been the Shovelhead, probably because most of my first years

You can tell these are factory photos by looking at the paint scheme that flows from the bike over the top of the helmets of the two riders. I'm not sure why the girl on this 1973 Super Glide is smiling, as it looks like her partner has taken up the whole seat, leaving her to straddle the fender.

with motorcycles were spent trying to fix one old worn-out Harley after another, and I never owned a bike that would run more than two days in a row until my finances allowed me to be owned by a brand shiny-new 1982 FXRS fitted with the last-generation Shovelhead motor.

Shovels had been around in one guise or another for 16 years prior to my purchase, so I wasn't exactly taking a wild chance by signing up for three years of payments. Actually it was a fairly easy decision to buy a Shovelhead, as the last bike in my garage had been a 1980 Sportster—an instrument of torture to rival anything found in the Tower of London. When the Sporty was new, it ran a whole 300mi before the engine let go, and the bike had to be towed back to Sunnyvale

Harley-Davidson, near San Francisco. Four weeks later it was returned to me with the admonition to "Take it easy for the first 500mi; don't run the new engine above 3000rpm." This time it stayed away from the dealer for a whole 400mi—bad countershaft in the transmission, major oil leak. Seems as though there had been a batch of shafts improperly hardened from the supplier, and I had one of them. To the shop it went once more.

Seven days slid by, and my bike was mine again. Needless to say, I wasn't overcome with certitude as far as reliability went. However, this time all the parts seemed to want to stay in their rightful places for a while, so off I went on a tour.

Here's where I learned about engine vibration...wow, did that engine vibrate. Below

3000rpm—where I had run it for what seemed like 60 years—it ran fine, not smooth, but OK. Twist the throttle to anything above 3000, and it would vibrate so hard it put various parts of my anatomy (which shall remain nameless, but had to do with fathering children) to sleep. This bike and I were not destined to remain together much longer. When my friendly dealer announced the presence of an 80ci sport bike similar to the Super Glide, but with a rubber-mounted engine, called the FXRS, the Sportster's days were numbered. I think the Sportster was the only Harley-Davidson I ever unloaded with less than 2,000mi on the clock.

The Sporty's rapid replacement was due to a 20mi test ride spent on what was soon to be mine and the bank's new Shovelhead. The guys running Sunnyvale Harley-Davidson figured that letting me ride the new scoot would do the selling job for them. They were right. I wrote another check, signed a contract again, went back into more debt, and rode away happy.

I think I paid the grand total of $7,184, counting all government tariffs and anything else the shop could stack on the contract. One benefit— along with the bike—came a somewhat under-the-table credit for $200 worth of accessories. Also, I got to choose the color and paint scheme on the bike. It was all black originally, but I went for the black and orange that H-D's been using for years on their racing bikes. Took a whole two weeks to get the new fenders and tanks with the right paint. Try doing that today! These days just finding a new bike for sale is hard enough, let alone ordering one in your favorite colors. But in 1982, you could go down to your local dealer with a particular color on a sample chip, and H-D's paint shop would reproduce it on your new bike

Mountain View, California, 1966. Five Traffic Division motor cops get ready to go out and keep the streets safe. Four are on Shovelheads, while bike number six, ridden by the father of the man who gave me the photo, is a Panhead. *Forrest "Trees" Linderman*

within six weeks. As I said, things are a little different today. The factory still says they will custom-paint your bike, but the waiting list is so long that most people just take what rolls off the truck.

I still own the bike—matter of fact it's the only H-D I own—and hope to keep it, along with the new bike I have on order, for quite a few years. It's been stone-ax reliable, runs fine, and is totally housebroken. Matter of fact, the only time it has ever leaked oil was when we swapped the factory oil lines over to the metal braided type, and that was the line's fault, not the bike's. If the new bike shows up anytime soon, I'll just park the FXRS and keep it for hot sunny days.

Harley-Davidson has never been noted for rapid changes, and building the Shovel went right along with this leisurely philosophy. In the fall of 1965 they made what was for them a mighty design leap—they changed the cylinders and heads on the FLH. The Panhead had been soldiering along since shortly after the end of World War II—1948 to be exact—and after only 18 years, its time was up. When H-D engineers designed the Shovelhead, they kept the same basic cases and accessories as on the Pan, just went to the new cylinders and heads. The generator stayed in the same place, most everything else stayed as it was. The Panhead's Linkert carb only made it through the 1966 model year before disappearing off the engine. For 1967, the fuel and air mixed in a Tillotson carb, replete with its own fair share of problems, later to be replaced by a Bendix, equally cursed, and finally by a Keihin with its own set of interesting peccadilloes.

The early Shovel shared so many parts with the Pan that it wasn't uncommon to see Shovel top ends on Pan cases, or once in a while the other way around.

This 1968 FLH shows the optional long seat. As you can see by the H on the oil tank, this is the hotter-engined FLH (as opposed to the FL with 5hp less), drum brakes, white saddlebags, and all. Owned by Ernie Marietta from Northern California.

The early Shovels were actually a little bit slower than the kickstart Panheads, even though the Shovel was advertised as more powerful with 60hp, 5hp more than the Panhead. Most of this was due to added weight on the new bike. A 1952 FL tipped the scales at just under 600lb, while the 1966 Electra Glide pushed down with 780lb. A Pan even held about a 10mph speed advantage over the first Shovels. Things haven't changed much, as a stock 1994 California Evo, showing all of 39hp on the dyno at Custom Chrome's RevTech facility in Morgan Hill, California, won't get close enough to a Shovel to see its taillight in a drag race. The more things change…

The FLH had a sister bike—the FL—rated at 54hp. This engine was aimed at police departments and government agencies where reliability was thought to be more important than speed. Most police departments and government agencies took one ride on an FL and opted out for the FLH. They didn't like slow any more than the rest of us. The sales figures show the FLH outsold the FL by a vast majority.

These days, how fast an old Harley can go is mostly rhetorical, but the motorcycle magazines of the 1960s managed to get the FLH up to a thundering 98mph after a sufficiently long run. In today's world of 178mph Japanese plastic bikes, that top speed looks fairly slow; however, not many of us plan to flog our 20- to 30-year-old bikes up to warp speed any time soon. Besides "go fast" wasn't what these bikes were all about anyway. They were there to give you a ride on a real motorcycle—not one that leaked rice!

Trying to sort out the various and sundry models of the Shovelhead produced during its 19-year run can be quite confusing. Some of the bikes listed in the catalogs only appeared on paper, never on a dealer's floor. For instance, the 1972 model lineup showed an FLHF foot shift along with an FLH hand shift. This was the last year a hand shift was offered, and it's quite possible all of the 8,100 FLH bikes sold were sold as foot-shift only. The factory gamely advertised the bike with a foot clutch and tank-mounted shifter, but demand was nonexistent.

We will cover each model offered every year, even if it's only mentioned by type. For one person to keep track of all the different models produced over time would take a prodigious memory, and a real need to know. As mentioned, in 1972 both hand-shift and foot-shift bikes appeared in the catalog. They were listed as FLHF, FLH, FLPF, and FLP—"P" standing for "police." FLHF designates Electra-Glide with foot shift. In 1973 they eliminated most of the model designations, electing to go with just FL and FLH. The sales records for both years only show the bikes listed as FL and FLH, so the factory didn't differentiate too much when it came to actual accounting, except in 1974–75 where the police bikes were singled out as the FL Police. Sales of both types in 1973 amounted to 1,025 FLs and 7,750 FLHs, with the FX Super Glide selling 7,625 for a total sales of 16,400. Honda probably dropped more bikes off the boat while unloading that year.

Sales of the big bikes really didn't start to pick up substantially until the Evo made its appearance. Most sales figures back in the 1970s show a total of all Harleys sold, including Sportsters and the Italian bikes made by Aermacchi, to run right around 45,000–70,000 units, with the Sportster holding the top sales rung with most models sold. Then came changes.

The AMF Years

The 1970s saw a lot of changes for H-D. After being acquired by AMF in 1969, H-D had to walk the line chalked by a whole different group of suits. Some said joining with AMF was a good deal as H-D badly needed the influx of capital to update antique equipment and increase production. Some said lots of other things about the merger. Either way, the AMF logo appeared on all 1971 gas tanks and was there to stay through all the 1970s and up to the end of the 1981 model year.

During the AMF years, a lot of changes came about—some good, some not so good. Now that AMF Harley-Davidson existed, corporate changes tended to happen at the same rate steel rusts…as opposed to the glacial movement speed before the merger. Quality control went down the tubes while more government rules concerning noise and pollution appeared than ever before. Harley's engineering staff had to fight on two fronts, with most of the effort being applied to conforming to federal regulations. At the same time, the parent company decided to move most of H-D's opera-

Mike Quinn's 1971 FLH is about as stock as a 1971 FLH can be. The exhaust pipes don't even have any blue on them yet. That year, the throttle was changed to a twist grip with a single cable running to the carb but no return spring. Prior years had a spiral throttle with its cable running inside the bars. This was the year of the carb change from the venerable Tillotson to the Bendix/Zenith. *Nick Cedar*

tions from Milwaukee to an unused plant in York, Pennsylvania. This caused a lot of hard feelings among employees who lost jobs, and quality control further eroded.

Two sides exist to every story. AMF was a large business whose chief aim was to make money. Whether that was done by making motorcycles or lawn furniture, they didn't care. AMF really didn't have the slightest idea of how to run a motorcycle company, so it had to go through a learning curve while building Harleys. Unfortunately, sometimes this made the customer the final engineer for the bikes.

The immense boom in motorcycles also put a strain on AMF and H-D. Total sales went from 28,850 in 1970 to 75,403 in 1975 (22,245 being Big Twins, the balance being Sportsters and smaller Italian bikes). As a result, the factory equipment and people running that equipment were sorely taxed to keep quality in pace with production. The build quality dropped and sales suffered.

To give credit to AMF, if they hadn't come along in 1969 and taken H-D in tow, the Motor Company might only be a golf-cart manufacturer today. In 1969, sales revenues of all products were just over $49 million. When the turnover took place in 1981, sales had risen to $300 million. AMF's ownership of H-D wasn't all bad. Still, some of the bikes carry a stigma if an AMF logo appears on the tank.

As an example of some of the problems, most of the 1979 and 1980 bikes had to have the valve seats replaced within the first few thousand miles. Harley handled the problems under warranty, but the situation didn't do much for building customer satisfaction. The Japanese motorcycle manufacturers didn't help things much either when they flooded the market with bikes that were both inexpensive and reliable. For a while, it looked like H-D was going to join Henderson, Indian, and all the other defunct American brands if quality did not improve, and soon.

Note that the seat helper springs on this 1976 FLH are attached to the frame and the center post is disconnected. This gives the bike the two-step feeling when entering a turn. First the bike leans over...then the seat shifts over and falls into the direction of the turn, making the rider feel less than connected to what's going on below.

Here's a later model seat on a 1979 FLH. Not only is it more secure, but also it gives the passenger some semblance of a place to sit.

Things still didn't get much better when the 1981 models arrived. The biggest problem appeared on the 1981 FLHC, which left the factory with totally unbalanced flywheels. At the same time, engine knock due to lowered pump-gas octane got worse and could only be controlled by dropping the compression ratio to 7.4:1, dropping horsepower in the process. However, the owners didn't have to put up with massive vibration problems for long, as the bike usually shook hard enough to break down within a few thousand miles. This lack of quality, coupled with horsepower loss due to tightened emissions, brought H-D ever closer to the brink. Sales of the V-Twins in 1980 were 33,414, and in 1981 they fell to 31,504, a loss of 1,910 units.

Adios AMF

Problems continued with quality control at AMF H-D throughout the late 1970s and into the 1980s. Management and leadership were playing musical chairs without any chairs. Projects in the mill like the five-speed and Tour Glide didn't happen when planned. A recession was eating up the market. For the 1979–80 year sales of $280 million, H-D showed less than a $12 million profit.

Salvation was at hand. AMF decided to restructure its lineup of recreational companies and decided H-D was to go on the chopping block. Thence ensued a mad scramble of some of the upper management at AMF who were died-in-the-wool motorcycle crazies and figured they could buy H-D and turn the company around.

The only item that stood between Vaughn Beals, Richard Teerlink, and the hirsute Willie G. (all of whom should be canonized as far as I'm concerned) was the $75 million AMF wanted for H-D. AMF may have let quality go to hell and run sales to an all-time low, but they weren't going to let H-D go for free.

Beals, along with about 12 other totally aggravated colleagues, tubed AMF and went looking for a way to supplement $10 million of their own money with another $65 million needed to ransom H-D. Boy did they have a job of selling to do! Just about every lending agency rejected their requests. Finally, Citicorp cut a check to AMF for the needed funds, and Beals and company had a motorcycle business. Citicorp also got something out of the deal to the tune of $12 million per year for their generosity. Ever think you're in the wrong business? Move paper, make millions. Move wrenches and be damn glad to get $12 per hour. See, mom was right, you should have stayed in school and got that masters degree in business.

Later on, the company was able to arrange much better financing through the insurance syndicates. The day the AMF banner came down from the shops and off the bikes was celebrated all

No chain adjustments; no oil added!

FLT Tour Glides travel non-stop from Vancouver to Daytona!

When two Harley-Davidson FLT Tour Glide motorcycles rolled into Daytona Beach, Fla. the morning of March 3, they were the precise definition of the Harley-Davidson touring philosophy of comfort over the long haul, reliability and ease of maintenance.

The reason: only 78 hours earlier, the bikes were just leaving Vancouver, British Columbia, on a 3,850 mile virtual non-stop transcontinental journey.

The trip was made as a demonstration of that touring philosophy, but Harley-Davidson took it a couple of steps further. Unlike the average touring rider, who when eating and sleeping would no doubt park the motorcycle, the only time the engines on these vehicles were shut off was for refueling. In order to run the vehicles non-stop, riders were switched "Pony Express" style at approximate 200 mile intervals, with Harley-Davidson dealers and personnel handling the task. Additionally, absolutely no maintenance was performed en route, not even the routine maintenance prescribed in the vehicles' operating manual.

Prior to the trip, the Tour Glides received only normal preparation. Less than two weeks prior the ride's start, the motorcycles were pulled from the end of the York, Pa. assembly line and went through the company's normal audit procedures. They then received setup and preparation in accordance with the standard dealer preparation procedures. About 200 break in miles were put on the vehicles, after which they

were flown from York to Vancouver in time to start the run. Because the ride had been conceived and set in motion on extremely short notice, there was not even time to transport the motorcycles through more normal means.

There was, however, one non-standard "accessory" outfitted on each vehicle — a sealed oil tank. At York, the engine oil filler cap was sealed, as were the transmission and chain oil filler openings, meaning that if any oil was added, the seals would have to be broken. The motorcycles arrived in Daytona, seals intact. When the oil tanks were later topped off to determine consumption, 1.4 qts. were added to one vehicle, 1.6 qts. to the other, for an average of 2,578 miles per quart. Thus, refueling was the only activity, other than riding, for the entire 3,850 mile trip. *Not even the chains were adjusted!*

The trip itself covered all types of terrain, through all kinds of conditions, from mile-high elevations to sea level. High winds, rain and cold were common. At times, road speeds dropped to 15 mph to negotiate fog and icy conditions, and climbed above speed limits to make up lost time.

In total, 39 riders participated in the non-stop transcontinental trip, which followed U.S. Interstate highways I-5 and I-10 to Jacksonville, Fla. Harley-Davidson Chairman Vaughn L. Beals, and company President Charles K. Thompson, climbed aboard at Jacksonville for the final leg down I-95 to Daytona Beach.

Harley-Davidson President Charlie Thompson (left) and Chairman Vaughn Beals, complete the transcontinental, non-stop motorcycle ride by touching the FLTs' wheels to the Daytona sand.

Harley-Davidson President Charlie Thompson (left) and Chairman Vaughn Beals completed a 3,806mi transcontinental ride on two 1980 FLT Tour Glides from Vancouver, Canada, to Daytona Beach, Florida, on March 3, 1980. The ride involved 39 riders and took 78 hours to run. Neither bike had any adjustments, and the oil tanks were sealed on both FLTs. Oil mileage averaged 2,578 miles per quart. *Harley-Davidson*

over the country. Harley now only had to pay back the loan, turn around quality, improve the morale of the workers, and make a profit. The last ten years have shown the results. Harley has moved from being a rolling joke to being the most desired vehicle in the world. None of this would have happened without a lot of very hard work on the part of the people of H-D. Everybody from Richard Teerlink and Vaughn Beals, down to the guy who sweeps up the metal shavings, made the company what it is today.

Going Uphill

First though, H-D had to play catch-up with their products. They were headed in the proper direction with the Super Glide and its spin-offs but were still being hounded by government regulations.

In 1982 H-D—minus AMF—came out with an updated model of the FX series, called the FXRS, sporting a rubber-mounted engine, a new oil-control package, and a five-speed transmission. The big touring FLTs already had the benefits of rubber engine mounts, but they used a frame that wouldn't work on the FX bikes, so a new one was designed to take the 80ci motor and five-speed while still retaining the Super Glide look.

The people at the factory got their act together, and quality on the last few years of Shovelheads was much improved. By the time of its replacement by the Evo in mid-1984, the Shovel was quite a reliable motor, capable of running for 50,000–60,000mi without major repair— a big change from engines of the previous decade.

All of Harley-Davidson's corporate officers gather for a cross-country ride to celebrate the 75th anniversary in 1978. Vaughn Beals is on the FLH with the "75th Anniversary" sticker on the front fender; Willie G. is to his left. Charlie Thompson is on the Electra Glide behind Willie G. *Harley-Davidson*

Throughout the Shovelhead years, sales of the big bikes stayed consistently around the 7,000-per-year range during the 1960s, only climbing over 10,000 after the FX series began in 1971. In 1981, the FX bikes outsold the FLs 22,708 to 8,796. Clearly, the factory-chopper look was taking over in popularity. Now, anyone could have what appeared as a custom bike without having to spend months tearing down an FLH and investing thousands of dollars in aftermarket parts.

So, years 1966 to 1984 saw the Shovelhead go through many incarnations. It started out as a kickstart with electric backup, four-speed, 74ci Milwaukee vibrator, and ended up a smooth, five-speed, 80ci, reliable machine.

The Bikes in the Book

For the most part, the bikes appearing in this book belong to people who ride them frequently—weather permitting or not. Shovels haven't been new for eleven years, so finding one that hasn't had something changed—even something as small as a turn signal—is hard to do. These are the bikes you ride. These aren't factory-prepared show bikes—they're the ones you, the readers, have owned and put a lot of money, time, and affection into keeping on the road.

Buying a Shovelhead

Be advised that there are a few semi-talented people out in Harley land that might try to pass off something as what it isn't—like a factory hand-shift 1973 FLH. Now this is a fairly rare bike, as the factory didn't build any, but the parts do exist to make one up. You might still buy it, as long as you are aware of what it is. In a few years it might even be worth a couple of bucks more just because it's a Harley, but don't lay money on it. Take the time to look carefully at what you are trying to buy. If possible, take along someone who knows enough about Shovels to recognize a phony and is disinterested enough to keep you from spending money if you catch a case of "gotta-have-its."

If the one item that makes the bike more valuable looks fairly new compared to all the rest of the bike—beware. Try to take the bike to a dealer for a pre-purchase inspection, just as is done with airplanes. Any reputable owner won't object to you having an inspection done by a Harley-authorized shop, providing you pay all expenses. Should he resist an inspection by the pros and you can't live without the bike, be sure to check it carefully and definitely ride it before handing over more than a deposit. If you do buy it, and then find problems after you've owned it for a few weeks, don't feel alone; we've all done the same thing at least once. Hold onto this thought—the old Romans even had the same problem—their motto was *caveat emptor*…buyer beware.

All the mounted motorcycle force of Louisville, Kentucky, join for a picture on their Shovelheads at the finish line of historic Churchill Downs horse track. More horsepower is gathered on the infield than ever saw a race. This picture was taken in the late 1970s, sometime after 1977.

Investment?

Above all, buy what you want and enjoy it. If it's your first Harley, you'll learn more about motorcycles and people than you ever thought possible. And I fully believe that *all* Shovels will appreciate in value as they age and the price of new Harleys goes up, so your money's safe. I just came from my dealer in San Jose, where I spent some time lusting after one of their touring machines again. To give you an idea as to where prices are going, check this: A pre-sold blue 1995 FLHTC sitting on their showroom floor, replete with all the factory chrome, stereo radio, and even catalytic converters, but no dealer-installed options, runs:

Base 1995 FLHTC: $14,518

Freight and prep: $745 (a lotta bucks for a truck ride and a wax job)

California license and registration: $344

Doctor fee (maybe medical?): $35

Sales tax@8.25 percent (eek!): $1,262.09

Grand Total: $16,404.09

Figure a down payment of 10 percent is $1,650, and your $348 payments only run sixty months.

A lot of people have said that the cowboy never vanished, he just turned into the Harley rider. Judging by this picture, that could be quite true.

I asked about a deal—what with being a writer and all; plus I've known these people since I helped build their back shop area nine years ago. Rich, the salesman, said if the guy who laid down the deposit dropped out of the sale he'd knock the $.09 off the price, making it an even $16,404. He said all the bikes except for *one* Ultra Classic Electra Glide ($20,000 plus) are sold up through the first six months of 1996. He just quit taking deposits after that point.

Now you are probably reading this shortly into 1996, so you have in your hand what I'm writing in November of 1995. I doubt seriously things will get any better any time this century as far as availability, and lack of new scooters will do nothing but drive the price of clean older bikes upward. How high can prices go? Remember, the new 1964 FLH Panhead went out the door for the princely sum of $1,673; a 1967 FLH could be had for $2,100. Today, one 1966 FLH that belongs to a Federal Express corporate pilot in Memphis recently changed hands for $12,000. He has a 1971 FLH that can be yours for $10,000. If it's like the 1966, it will go away at the first phone call.

I paid $6,900 base price for my 1982 FXRS in December of 1981, and I hope, if I have to sell it to own the new bike, it goes away for close to $10k, 'cause you can guess why I'm real aware of the exact price of a 1995 FLHTC. Yup, and I'm going to have to wait for a 1996 that won't even be built until mid-May, six months from now, so I'll be paying even more when it arrives. I don't really want to part with the FXRS, and hope to be able to hang on to it, but as I said in my last book on performance Big Twins, I needed a touring bike to get out to the people who do the building and riding. My 1982 FXRS will be retired when the new bike arrives, and only sold if a large profit can be realized. Do I think Shovels are a smart investment? Is a bear Catholic?

To celebrate the Nation's Bicentennial, Harley issued a special edition called the "Liberty Edition" of the FLH-1200. Paint was black metallic, the seat was black also, and decals commemorating the event adorned the fairing, tanks, and top bag. This 1976 Liberty poses at the National Cemetery in Phoenix, Arizona.

PART ONE

The 1966—84 FL Series

In order to really talk about the first Shovelhead, the 1965 Panhead—from which the new motor was derived—needs to be described. This way the progression from the older engine to the Shovelhead becomes clear.

The last Panhead hit the shops in 1965. By then it had come a long way from the first 61ci and 74ci bikes of the late 1940s and early 1950s. The 1965 Pan sported an electrical starter—the second production Harley to do so, the first being the 1946 Servicar. The electrical system got a bump up from six-volt to 12-volt, and a heftier battery was included to help turn through the engine. Now that it started with a button, a new name was in order. Harley christened the new bike the Electra-Glide in obvious reference to its new capabilities. Later years saw the hyphen between "Electra" and "Glide" disappear. The first photos of a 1965 FLH Electra-Glide show the now-standard left foot shift, hand clutch, and button on the right handlebar that engaged the starter. Optional equipment, which many ordered, included dual mufflers, saddlebags, solo windshield, rear package rack, more

The Shovelhead engine powered all big Harleys from 1966 to 1984, in 74ci and 80ci sizes. This is the "generator motor" with the ignition timer mounted on a shaft in front of the number-one cylinder push-rod cover. *Harley-Davidson*

The Shovelhead first appeared in 1966. The head was new, but the cases were basically straight off the Panhead engine. This 1966 FLH is a highly polished stock machine. New for 1966, the six-sided Harley-Davidson emblem replaced the bar-type used on the Panhead. The new emblem would be around through 1971. *Doug Mitchell*

chrome trim on the fender, and case guards. Unfortunately, the larger battery and the existing swingarm rear suspension took up some of the room occupied by the black oblong toolbox, which had been mounted on the right side of the frame in front of the shock. The toolbox left, never to return as a factory installation. Nowadays a similar toolbox, black or chrome, is offered as an option for some of the current models.

The engine was still the same overhead valve (OHV) V-twin of 74ci as the prior year. Power stayed at an advertised 60hp, but now it had the job of pushing almost 790 unladen pounds down the road. This was quite a weight gain from earlier models without all the electrics. The early 1950s

Pan weighed right around 600lb; however, this was before the bike was given rear suspension (1958) and without all the options so dearly loved by owners.

The Electra Glide Panhead stayed around only one year before H-D changed the engine for the 1966 model to what has become known as the Shovelhead.

Motorcycle magazines in the 1960s sometimes didn't exactly report how things really were with products they road-tested. If pressed against the wall, they would admit that vibration in Harleys was a little, ever so tiny, insignificant, small problem. The need to clamp a piece of inner tube between your teeth over 60mph was a totally unfounded rumor (although I have the chipped teeth to prove it).

Now, I'm not sure who built their test bike, but it obviously wasn't the same gnomes who put together the 1963 Panhead I used to own. Mine was box stock, no trick pipes, no black paint with death's heads on the tanks. I worked for Boeing Aircraft in Seattle at the time, and my shift started at six-in-the-dark AM. I wasn't smart enough to drive a car when the weather went bad—rain was considered just a normal day—so every morning at 5:00 AM, I was out in the driveway kicking the bike alive. Just retard the spark, crack the throttle, click on two notches of choke, turn the engine through a couple of times with the ignition off, set the choke fully closed, light the ignition, and kick.

Easy, huh?

Sometimes it took one kick to fire—sometimes the helmet, jacket, shirt, and gloves were on the

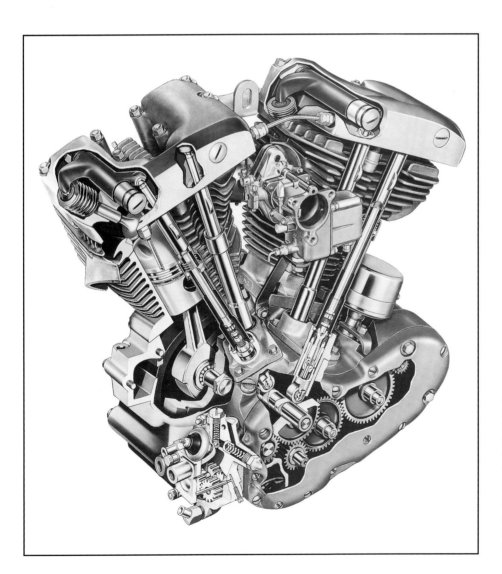

A cutaway of the same motor shows valve operation all the way from the cam, through the roller tappets, via the push rods and through the rockers to the valve. The oil-pump gears also can be clearly seen at the back of the engine. *Harley-Davidson*

ground by the time it lit off. Then it had to warm up, of course, or else it'd die when the clutch first went home—five minutes at the least before it could move under its own power. Being 18 years old (stupid), I usually managed to use a lot more throttle than necessary when leaving to show my appreciation for easy-starting bikes.

Two weeks of this, with my "silent"Harley, and the neighbors dropped by to mention capital punishment, ropes in trees, and other unpleasant outcomes if I didn't cease and desist with the noise. I ended up having to push the bike almost one block away before I could start the engine. Then it was a hurried 70mph ride to Boeing's Renton plant so as not to be late. One of the most welcome updates H-D ever made was adding electric start to their Big Twin.

1966 Electra Glide: The First Shovelhead

Production
    FLH (both models): 5,625
        FLHFB: 74ci foot-shift Super Sport
        FLHB: 74ci hand-shift Super Sport
    FL (both models): 2,130
        FLFB: 74ci foot-shift
        FLB: 74ci hand-shift

Along about 1965, Harley-Davidson decided, in its usual way, to make improvements on the Panhead. Normally, H-D changed a little bit each year, with the frame and suspension getting upgraded one year, and the motor the next. For the 1966 model year, the engine got

Spin the motor around and this is what the drive side looks like. The generator is mounted to the front of the engine, just below the ignition timer and is gear-driven off the engine. *Harley-Davidson*

the upgrades. Instead of putting a cover over the rockers on top of the engine, as on the Panhead, now the Shovel had real rocker boxes with the rockers mounted in them. When viewed from the side, the rocker boxes had the shape of a coal shovel, hence the name Shovelhead. To those of you under 35, coal is a black, greasy rock burned to make heat—kinda like diesel oil in hunks. Coal got from the coal bin in the basement to the furnace with a shovel of a particular shape. Looked at upside down, the coal shovel bore a resemblance to the new top end.

New parts included rocker housings, rockers and shafts, push rods, exhaust valves, and a few other small parts. The rest of the engine—intake valve, valve springs, hydraulic lifters, and all the rest carried forward from the Pan. The right crankcase was modified, the oil-feed port moved from between the lifter guides to behind the rear lifter guide. Cylinders stayed the same, the generator still rode in front, the carb changed to a Linkert model DM for this year only. Other than that, the motor was unchanged. The engines were so similar that Shovel top ends would easily fit a set of Pan cases.

Frames

When Harley-Davidson started producing Electra Glides with new and improved starters and bigger batteries, they found out that the frame would have to be opened up in the center section in order to fit all the bigger electrics within. If you look at an Electra Glide frame, and a Duo-Glide frame. the differences become apparent. Other than that, the frames fitted to the first Shovelheads are similar enough to where a Pan engine will fit into a Shovel frame, and versa visa.

The Shovel used the same rear frame section that the Panheads had in 1965. However, the shocks were still mounted way too far forward to provide adequate control for the rear swingarm, which in turn let the rear wheel wander under high loads. This was done so that law enforcement agencies and touring riders had enough room to mount saddlebags, radio gear, riot batons, shotguns, and all the other necessities of motorcycle riding.

Having the rear dampers set so far down, the swingarm gives the bike some rather unpleasant handling characteristics that show up at the worst possible time. This can be seen when following an early FLH into a turn. The rear wheel seems to take on a life of its own, running and hopping from side to side as the rider stuffs the bike into a turn.

Even though cornering isn't the big bikes' strong suit, if all is right with the suspension it can be bent around at a surprising rate of speed for a bike that weighs more than a sack of anvils. Some of this is due to the bike feeling like its center of gravity is 2ft below ground. The rest is due to the bike's ability to get you through the corner no matter how many parts are grinding off below. Those that hurry an FLH tend to replace floor boards rather frequently.

Today, the handling of the FL series isn't much better or worse than your average Gold Wing, but back in 1967 the only other bikes for comparison were Triumphs—which went around corners well enough to prove England is full of crooked roads—and the occasional Bultaco 250cc or Ducati of the same size, either of which would leave the bigger bikes for dead at the first hint of a wiggle in the road. The Japanese bikes available at the time—Kawasaki 350 Avengers and Suzuki 500s—usually had the advantage of acceleration, even if they handled like a goat on roller-blades.

A small part of the cornering problem was brought on by the original Goodyear 5.10x16in tires mounted front and rear. Goodyear said the tires were designed especially for H-D, and in some respects they were right. The tires were fairly abrupt in transition due to their rather sharp tread-to-sidewall angle. They really wanted to go in a straight-line like a car tire. When called upon to lean over, they hesitated before making the transition from straight line travel to a lean angle. Riding an early Shovel fitted with the stock Goodyears was an extremely steady experience on the California freeways. I can remember clearly setting the throttle to a good cruising speed, then sliding back on the seat to the grab rail and hanging my boots over the passenger pegs. I'd sit tall, with my arms folded tight against my leather jacket, watching people watching me. My friend, whom I felt seriously needed mental care, would sit all the way back on the luggage rack of his bike and wave at passing cars (kids don't try this at home).

And here's the bike with the engine fitted. The 1966 Electra Glide was the first Shovelhead. Some optional equipment is shown on this bike—saddlebags, windshield, crash bars, and seat among the main items. *Harley-Davidson*

The point is that, other than I'm probably very lucky to be able to write this book, the bike was extremely reluctant to move from a straight path. Part of this was due to the weight and frame design, part to the square-section tires.

Later in the year, after one particular frog-strangler of a storm, we took both bikes up a dirt road in the Santa Cruz Mountains and played "fall down." We could only get up to 20mph or so before the street tires slid out in a spray of mud, so no one was hurt when the bike's went over. I fell twice, and he went down three and a half times. The tires would slowly slide out to one side or the other, and the bike would lay down on its crash bars in the glop like a farm pig in a mud wallow. We finally had to give up and turn around when

the bikes flat wouldn't go any farther, but were both laughing so hard that we dropped them both again. No damage was done, other than mud everywhere. Guys on Maicos and Husqvarnas sure looked at us funny, though.

Harley suggested 20psi tire pressure in the front and 24psi in the back when riding solo. Actually, 30psi helped a lot more toward making the bike handle in the turns. I'd crank the bike into a particularly nasty, decreasing-radius turn, and no matter how much metal was throwing sparks, the bike would always track through the corner like a motorized anvil. Admittedly, the speed was a lot slower than that of the rice-rockets; however, we traveled stately, nary a wobble in sight. Now all this went out the window should you lean a little too far into the turn to where the muffler became the main source of traction instead of the rear wheel. At that point, life became much more interesting as the rear end stepped out one or two feet in a resounding hop. Once the rear rubber regained touch with the road, everything worked right again—but this made for a few tense moments indeed. As my failing memory tells me, I think the bike would ride up on the muffler easier when turning right than left—might have been me though. I was always more hesitant to go rubbing parts briskly upon the tarmac when turning left at oncoming traffic as opposed to having nothing but the odd lamppost to kiss while turning to the right.

Other changes

Small, but important changes to the rest of the bike included moving the fuel shut-off valve, operated by screwing down to shut off the flow, from its place on the top of the Panhead's left gas tank in front of and to the side of the speedometer. Now a petcock hung from under the left tank. The steel line connecting the two tanks became rubber. The ignition timer featured a new clamp.

The tank emblem changed to a six-sided metal item with the name "Harley-Davidson" embossed down the middle. This emblem stayed on the tanks through 1971. The rounded "half-moon" foot boards, in use since 1940, gave way to a new rectangular design. This was the last year of the round air filter and cover, pointed fender tips, and optional fishtail mufflers. Paint on the tank was two-tone, primary color underneath a white panel down the side. Wide at the front, the white panel tapered down to a rounded point at the bottom rear of the tanks. It had a 1/2in stripe, separate from the main. A similar colored 1/2in stripe, separated by a 1/4in gap, outlined the white panel. Black, Indigo Metallic, Hi-Fi Blue, gold, and Sparkling Burgundy were among the colors offered for 1966. Model designation included the letter "B" to designate electric start.

This 1966 FLH sports the buddy seat with two helper springs attached and a back support rail. Aside from a little too much chrome and polishing of the aluminum, it's close to what they looked like stock. *Doug Mitchell*

Left
The rear shot clearly shows the narrowness of the FLH. This 1966 has the optional bags and guards. The back rack took an optional top bag called a "Tour-Pak." *Nick Cedar*

In 1967, a fully optioned FLH looked like this one in Rapid City, South Dakota. Some of the readily apparent options include the centerstand, turnout mufflers, and windshield and bags. The pad behind the buddy seat is colored to match the red on the optional two-tone paint scheme. *Field Communications*

New for 1966, the six-sided Harley-Davidson emblem replaced the bar-type used on the Panhead. The new emblem would be around through 1971. *Field Communications*

The FLH's rear crash bars came off the top shock mount, out past the saddlebags, and attached underneath the shock. You can see why there is a cover over the top of the left header pipe—it was much too easy to lay the inside of a leg against it when riding. The "H" on the oil tank designates the more powerful FLH engine. *Field Communications*

This convention would disappear in the 1970 model year.

At the time of the Shovelhead's introduction, H-D improved the wiring system and added an improved electric foot. The kickstarter still remained, which was good because the early starters, said to have been developed from a boat outboard motor unit, came with their share of problems.

The oil pump was a steel unit. The intake manifolds were O-ringed on to a spigot screwed into the heads, eliminating one source of leaks. The heads had improved oil-return passages, helping with oil control. In earlier engines, oil could be pumped into the rocker covers faster than it could drain back, sometimes causing leaks or running past the valve guides and out the exhaust.

The bar brace across the handlebars of this fully optioned 1967 FLH is a seldom seen option. This was the last year for the older style Panhead instrument console. Both tanks had to be filled when gas was added. There is a rubber crossover line that replaced the 1965 metal line under the tanks, but its small diameter precludes filling one tank and letting the levels equalize. *Field Communications*

Front crash bars bolted to the upper frame between the downtubes. The lower end ran down and bolted on in front of the new rectangular foot boards. *Field Communications*

One of Mike Quinn's bikes again. This 1966 FLH marks the first year of Shovelhead production.
Nick Cedar

During the first year of production, 5,625 Shovelhead FLHs rolled out of the factory. Another 2,130 low-compression motors were fitted into the FL bikes. The FL was intended as a police and government bike, used also for low-speed duties such as escort work and accompanying someone on their last drive in a funeral procession. The lower compression of the FL motor cost it 5–6hp, in the name of reliability and lack of heating problems. Of course, performance dropped an equivalent amount, too. Most agencies opted for the faster bike over the reliability. What the cops didn't want was a bike with less performance than the one the public could buy off the showroom floor. The stock FLH, full of gas, creaked onto the scales at a hefty 785lb—top speed, after a half-mile run, was 98mph.

The new Shovel was a lot more civilized than kickstart-only bikes. It didn't require the services of a gorilla who was part magician to kickstart the bike. The FLH, replete with touring package—new and thicker windscreen, saddlebags, deluxe seat, supplementary lights, and extra chrome trim—became the ultimate in touring machines. Coupled with improved reliability, it heralded a new era in riding.

The 1966 engine had the engine timer mounted in a case on the right side of the engine, in front of the first push rod tube. The early engine cases were unfinished aluminum without any decoration or logos. You can see by the size of the kickstarter that a healthy foot was needed to urge this engine into life if the battery died. *Nick Cedar*

Below
The rear exhaust pipe could easily come in contact with a passenger's leg; therefore, the chrome cover just under the oil tank. The "H" on the oil tank designated the more powerful FLH engine. *Nick Cedar*

The Competition

Looking back at a 1966 FLH, it doesn't seem anywhere as sophisticated as what is available today. However, compared to what else was available back then, it was miles ahead. A 1966 Triumph Bonneville or Honda 305 Superhawk might be able to out pull the FLH up to 60mph, but riding a motorcycle isn't just stoplight drag races. Big-bike riders wanted to get from place to place in comfort. They didn't give a tinker's damn about ultimate performance as long as there was enough to pull two people and luggage down the road at 70mph. In this, the FLH Shovelhead excelled.

Prior to the introduction of the Shovelhead, H-D had been fighting competition from England in the form of 500cc and 650cc vertical twins from Triumph, BSA, Norton, and others. Along with these bikes, 500cc singles from companies like Matchless, AJS, and BSA, were giving H-D's dirt track racers a bad time. The Triumphs, in particular, were giving H-D fits on the street. Not only did they start so easily that the kickstarter could be pushed through by hand, but also they would leave a Panhead for dead in any speed contest. Meanwhile, on a good day, the BSA 500cc Goldstars could actually win a race or two from the H-D 750cc flathead flat-trackers that ran in American Motorcycle Association (AMA) sanctioned Class C dirt-track racing. And back then the AMA meant *American* motorcycles, with the rules weighed heavily to favor H-D's antiquated side-valve KRs.

The 650cc Triumphs and BSAs could and would do anything an 883cc Sportster could do—plus they made pretty good sport-touring bikes long before the term was coined. The British invasion started cutting seriously into H-D's sales around the time of the 1958 Triumph 650cc Thunderbird, and continued through such bikes as the 1970 Triumph Bonneville and the BSA Lightning. By this time, the Japanese were building up their production of 450cc to 750cc bikes, and when the British slowly sank into the sunset with their last efforts, the Triumph Trident and BSA Rocket—two 750cc three-cylinder bikes that really went nowhere—the next wave of imported bikes like Honda, Kawasaki, Yamaha, and Suzuki were well on their way to dominating the market.

The general feeling during the late 1950s and early 1960s was that total motorcycle sales for any year, all makes and models counted, would never rise above 100,000. It had been so for years, and no one could see how it could ever change. The idea of an Asian country, especially one who had lost a war with us not too long ago, flooding the market with hundreds of thousands of inexpensive, small- and medium-size motorcycles was unthinkable. The British would continue sending us Triumphs, Nortons, BSAs, and Matchlesses, which would continue to vibrate, break cranks, and die in the most remote places possible. Harley would continue to build bikes that leaked oil, shook like a blender full of ball bearings, and distributed parts blissfully down the road at regular intervals. The status would stay quo.

Planning a ride of 1,000mi was a true adventure back then. The few cycle books of the time carried tales of how some brave soul took a motorcycle across the Northern Sahara desert with only two stops to replace the rings or rebuild the carburetor. He crossed in less than three weeks and only lost 23lb in the process—oh yeah, and one case of heat prostration, but he considered that only normal. Flat tires weren't even mentioned; they just were part of the ride. Today, we'd be hard put to even have a light bulb break on the same trip without calling the service department on our cellular phone. New bikes today have the life expectancy of your average family sedan—100,000mi, or 10 years between tear downs. The good old days of motorcycling are today.

The good old days—no helmets, bare legs, and a brand new 1966 FL to tour the countryside with your lady on back. This was obviously the best way to travel. *Harley-Davidson via Buzz Buzzelli*

This Hi-Fi Red and White 1966 Electra Glide, owned by Rick Newman, was the 206th FLH Shovelhead produced. This one has a few trick options: a custom horn cover on the left side of the engine, two-tone windshield, and steering damper for the front forks (mostly used on sidecar bikes). It also has some large chrome trim pieces covering the electrics and the back half of the bike. *Jeff Hackett*

Everything from the mousetrap to the cover in front of the rear shock has either been polished, or chromed, except for the primary case cover. The bag mounted above the bars was an option for that year. The Panhead had a fuel shutoff valve in front of the left gas cap; the Shovel has it moved off the tank and down under the left side. *Jeff Hackett*

This is what a box-stock 1967 FLH looked like, fresh off the factory floor or, as in this case, fresh off the restorer's floor. Look closely at the left side and you can see the "mousetrap" clutch spring and mount on the front frame downtube. *Jeff Hackett*

1967 Electra Glide

Production
    FLH (all): 5,600
            FLHFB: 74ci foot-shift Super Sport
            FLHB: 74ci hand-shift Super Sport
            FLH: 74ci hand-shift
    FL (all): 2,150
            FLFB: 74ci foot-shift

In the second year of Shovelhead production, H-D changed the oil ring on the pistons back to a cast-iron model instead of the three-piece and expander they had been using prior to this. Turns out that the oil rings were outlasting the rest of the engine. Also, break-in tended to take too many miles, and too much oil slipped passed while the ring was breaking in. The replacement ring did an adequate job of keeping oil out of the combustion chamber and allowed the friction surfaces between it and the cylinder to mate rapidly, which reduced oil consumption. Somewhat a case of one part being built too well.

The old Linkert Model DC gave way to a Tillotson pumper carb. This had an accelerator pump as part of the carb. When the throttle was twisted, the pump gave a shot of gas right away. Most other carbs of the time relied on air velocity through the carb venturi to create enough vacuum to lift some fuel out of the float bowl. A quick shot of raw fuel ensured easier starts and faster throttle response while underway.

The venerable fishtail mufflers were replaced by a new, optional "turnout" type muffler. The rear brake drum was updated along with its axle and wheel spacer. The only other changes on the bike were cosmetic, like new rectangular fender tips (another optional extra) and a few other small pieces. Paint remained similar to the 1966 bikes, except that the white panel tapered to a point at the rear of the tank. Standard colors were Black and Crystal Blue. Optional colors were Sparkling Burgundy and Hi-Fi Blue.

This two-toned 1967 FLH has a white panel on the tank where the 1968s had the crackle finish.
Jeff Hackett

The "ham can" air cleaner cover is a change from the round cover used in 1966. Note the unpolished gear-cover case below the carburetor. This is correct for restoration, and how the cover came from the factory. *Jeff Hackett*

1968 Electra Glide

Production
    FLH (all models): 5,354
        FLHFB: 74ci foot-shift Super Sport
        FLHB: 74ci hand-shift Super Sport
    FL (all models): 1,718
        FLFB: 74ci foot-shift
        FLB: 74ci hand-shift

This FLH has just about all the options. Whitewall tires to fishtail pipes, it even comes with a centerstand. I think the two-tone seat is a nice touch.

The major internal engine change for 1968 was the replacement of the steel-bodied oil pump with an aluminum-bodied pump featuring new pressure-feed gears. The starter problems were finally rectified by 1968. The starter now came from Homelite and was more than fit for the job of turning over two cylinders of 37ci each. The starter used an automotive-type Bendix spring operating through a pinion to engage the ring gear on the clutch. The 12-volt battery was uprated to 53amp-hr, making for easier cold-morning starts and allowing all the various electrical accessories and lights that some owners were so fond of hanging on the bike.

Outside the engine, the one part conspicuous by its absence was the clutch mousetrap. Previous years' foot-shift bikes had a clutch booster mounted under the left tank on the front down tube. Its purpose was to aid the left hand while pulling in the clutch, which took a bit of muscle as the clutch

Elsewhere in this book you'll see some more of Mike Quinn's bikes. Among others, he owns this immaculate 1967 red FLH with optional turnout mufflers. *Nick Cedar*

About the only thing not stock on the 1967 FLH are the highway pegs mounted on the crash bars. *Nick Cedar*

The front fender of this 1967 FLH sports an emblem and chrome rail, both optional in that year. *Nick Cedar*

Below
In 1967, both hand- and foot-shift versions of the FLH were available. This version is, obviously, one of the more popular foot-shirt varieties. *Nick Cedar*

was the same as the one used when the pedal was operated by a much stronger leg.

Under a cover was an over-center spring that aided in the clutch pull once the handlebar lever was pulled in about one inch. The clutch cable from the handlebar lever went to this mousetrap instead of the actual clutch. From there, a rod operated the clutch release arm. This was of significant help when trying to hold in the clutch at a stoplight, but made for somewhat a strange feeling as the lever was let out. There was a definite feel when the mousetrap went to work pulling the clutch in; coming out, a rider could actually feel the boost of the spring working to push the lever out. A new clutch release arm, cable, and linkage replaced the mousetrap and its operating rod. Now a cable went all the way from the clutch lever on the handlebar to the clutch release arm.

The speedometer housing received the biggest cosmetic change that year. Gone were the three separate round indicator light lenses between the alarm clock speedometer and the rotating ignition switch. The replacement panel sported three rectangular lenses aligned in a strip between the speedometer and the ignition switch. From the left, the indicator lights were for high beam, neutral, and oil pressure. This dash

The paint on the 1968 Electra Glide was two-toned with the center portion being a black crackle finish, as shown on this tank. The engine side cases have been highly polished. This was done by the owner, as H-D was into the "agricultural implement" look at the time and didn't polish anything. Even the wheel spokes were just painted silver.

continued on all FL and FLH (not the five-speed FLHT) up to 1984. It also did duty on the 1971–71 FX models and 1980–84 Wide Glide.

The standard gas tanks were rated at 3.5gal, with 5gal tanks optional.

Paint schemes took a strange turn with the middle white panel being replaced with a black crackle finish. Standard colors included Black and Jet Fire Orange. Optional colors included Sparkling Burgundy and Sparkling Blue. Some very late production bikes had the tank colors divided longitudinally with the base color on top, separate by a white stripe from the crackle finish, the emblem mounted in the white stripe.

This 1968 FLH was one of 5,354 FLHs produced that year. The lower power of the FL made it less popular, and only 1,718 FLs were built in 1968. *Nick Cedar*

1969 Electra Glide

Production
> FLH (all models): 5,500
>> FLHFB: 74ci foot-shift Super Sport
>> FLHB: 74ci hand-shift Super Sport
> FL (all models): 1,800
>> FLFB: 74ci foot-shift
>> FLB: 74ci hand-shift

No major mechanical changes were seen for the 1969 model year. Cosmetically, the old optional Plexiglas windscreen was joined by an optional handlebar-mounted white fiberglass fairing. It enclosed the headlight and turned with the bars. This set a style that was to last a quarter-century. Along with the fairing, the owner had the option of ordering a complete touring package with saddlebags. A big fiberglass case could be mounted on the package rack on the rear fender. It was also colored white, like the fairing. The horizontally split paint scheme on the tank was featured for the 1969 year, including the black crackle lower paint and white center stripe. Standard colors included Black, Jet Fire Orange, and Birch White. Optional colors included Sparkling Burgundy, Sparkling Blue, and Sparkling Gold.

This was the last year for the chrome-plated flex-pipe header covers (optional to cover the painted header pipes). The generator and the external ignition timer also made their last appearances. The oil tank still carried an "FLH" decal, but next year, the decal would disappear.

This was the year AMF bought H-D.

1970 Electra Glide

Production

FLH (all models): 5,475
    FLHF: 74ci foot-shift Super Sport
    FLH: 74ci hand-shift Super Sport
FL (all models): 1,200
    FLPF: 74ci foot-shift, low-compression
    FL Police Special
    FLP: 74ci hand-shift, low-compression
    FL Police Special

This was the year for big engine changes. The generator, at its operational limit, departed, to be replaced by an alternator mounted inside the primary-chain case. The external ignition timer was

The 1968 FLH's tanks carried the same emblem as the previous year, but the new console appeared. Also note the slight change in design on the air cleaner cover.
Nick Cedar

This seat has an optional back pad giving the passenger something to brace against rather than holding on to the rider's coat or a bare back rail.
Nick Cedar

We should all be so lucky to own a 1969 FLH in this condition. *Nick Cedar*

deleted, and the points and auto-advance moved inside a new, cone-shaped gear-case cover. This was where the name "Cone Motor" was derived; motors prior to this design are called "generator motors."

The new timer is driven off the end of the cam gear, so the former timing gear is deleted from the gear case. New crankcases were fabricated, along with new inner and outer chain cases. The kick-starter was no more for the FL series. It wouldn't reappear until the FX series was introduced the following year.

In 1970, the four-speed FL primary cover had a different look. It had a hump at the front for the

This 1969 FLH has a windshield with the bottom half color-coded; however, a new bar-mount fairing was available. *Nick Cedar*

The year 1969 was the last year for the "generator" engine; the cone motor would appear in late 1969 as a 1970 model. *Nick Cedar*

alternator, a removable clutch inspection cover held on with three screws, and a sidestand bumper pad attached near the lower front of the outer primary. This cover carried on up to the 1984 model year on all four-speed FLs.

The header pipes now are chromed all the way to the mufflers, and the chrome-flex pipe header cover is no more. A new oil tank featured a dipstick that pulled out diagonally from the relocated fill hole near the tank's top left corner. The old tank's filler hole and dipstick resided under the seat.

One problem with the alternator engines; is that the engine was wider, and this pushed the floorboards out even more where they easily came in contact with the pavement.

From 1967–69, FLHs didn't change very much. This Alabama owner has added some rather interesting ends to the exhaust pipes and a little bit of chrome that wasn't from the factory, but other than that, the bike is stock. *Jeff Hackett*

Previous page
A 1969 Electra Glide in blue. The year 1969 was the last year for the chrome header pipe covers, generator, and external ignition circuit breaker. The rear shocks had to sit far forward on the swingarm to give room for the saddlebags. The battery sits under a chrome cover in front of the shock. *Jeff Hackett*

The Tillotson carb still fed the engine, and owners still bitched about the carb, but it was scheduled for replacement in the next year's model run.

The model designation methods changed in 1970. No longer was "B" used (as in FLHB, for designating electric start). Now a "P" was added

I thought this 1971 FLH deserved to be shown to the public. Not very often do you see a real saddle on a Harley. Tassels on the leather bags, leather thongs hanging from the bar ends, I'd say the owner is western oriented, wouldn't you? *Jeff Hackett*

to designate Police bikes whether they were hand-shifted or foot-shifted. The more powerful bikes were identified FLH and FLHF, depending on where the shifter resided.

The serial numbering convention changed also. Now year of manufacture was spelled out by using a letter for the decade and a number for the year. Hence a 1970 serial number would begin H0, H1 for 1971, H2 for 1972, and so on. This letter digit code is followed by another code for the model and the serial number.

1971 Electra Glide

Production
    FLH (all models): 5,475
        FLHF: 74ci foot-shift Super Sport
        FLH: 74ci hand-shift Super Sport
    FL (all models): 1,200
        FLPF: 74ci foot-shift, low-compression
        FL Police Special
        FLP: 74ci hand-shift, low-compression
        FL Police Special

Now this 1971 FLH is more to my liking. Wide whitewalls for the look, straight pipes for the sound, and a tall sissy bar to rest your favorite lady against while cruising the back roads of summer. *Jeff Hackett*

This is the year that the letters "AMF" first appeared on the tanks. Underneath, the new carb was a Bendix/Zenith to replace the Tillotson. (Actual changeover may have started late in the 1970 production run.)

1972 Electra Glide

Production
    FLH (all models): 8,100
        FLHF: 74ci foot-shift Super Sport
        FLH: 74ci hand-shift Super Sport
    FL (all models): 1,600
        FLPF: 74ci foot-shift, low-compression
      FL Police Special
        FLP: 74ci hand-shift, low-compression
      FL Police Special

Another of Mike Quinn's bikes, a totally stock 1971 FLH. The 1971 FLH had its throttle changed from the old-style "spiral," with control cable inside the right bar, to a more modern single-cable, twist grip with no return spring. This was the last year for the front drum brake and the six-sided tank emblem. *Nick Cedar*

The biggest change for 1972 was the changeover from a mechanically actuated front drum brake to a single hydraulically actuated disc; rear brakes were still drum. On bikes built prior to the disc brake installation, checking the right handlebar we encounter a lever. On some motorcycles, this is commonly referred to as the front brake lever; however, on the early FLH series it could only charitably be called a "speed-reducer" or "hill-holder." The front drum brake was an 8in by 1in drum, connected to the lever by a rather stout cable sufficient enough to secure a Lake Erie ore barge. All this is rather impressive looking, what with the big polished cover on the left side

of the wheel and all, but it has one minor drawback—it doesn't work. Once the brake lever is applied, the mechanical bits and pieces all do their job making the front fork bob up and down—that's about all they do, though. After the first hard application, the front lining and drum cease to have much friction between them, making braking action minimal at best. Pulling harder on the lever (be sure and sign up for a class in upper body improvement, concentrating on the arms and hands, prior to attempting this) adds slightly more retardation—usually much too late to be of any good. One should have matters firmly in hand and a good idea of stopping distances prior to rid-

Every front fender needs a bumper. This is what you got in 1971. Methinks the protection was secondary to the looks. *Nick Cedar*

Check the difference between this speedometer and the one on Rick Newman's 1966 a few photos back. This is the new style changed over in 1968. *Nick Cedar*

ing in a crowded city festooned with hills—like San Francisco, for instance.

In times of need, the rear brake can be called into play to aid the front binder. It's operated by a large black pedal attached to a piece of iron that looks like it served as a turn-signal mount on a German pocket battleship. All this connects to a hydraulic cylinder of distinctly automotive antecedents. Great leverage can be applied through the cylinder by the aforementioned lever-cum-pedal assembly, causing some rather interesting howls as the rear tire ceases to rotate. This does little to retard forward motion, however. The FLH is quite content to continue in a straight line with rear wheel rotation completely at a stop and the front end bobbing like a rubber duck in a bathtub on the *Queen Mary* on a stormy night. Thank God the bike tends to be stable no matter

what is done while riding.

If authenticity is your ultimate game and you don't wish to spoil the original lines of your pre-1972 Shovel by adding a front disc brake or two, you might consider taking the front brake shoes down to a reputable friction-material shop (listed in the *Yellow Pages* under Friction Material or Brakes) and see if they might have some of that old nasty metallic lining floating around. A particular brand that comes to mind is Velva-Touch, a lining with a lot of metal and a low rag content. At any rate, the gentlemen at the shop should be able to bond on a better quality lining than comes from the average aftermarket or H-D supplier.

One disadvantage to the metallic lining is that it requires a fair amount of heat to work properly. Warming the brakes prior to using them extensively helps a lot.

Just you and your significant other riding on that big white seat on a long summer's eve; enjoying the countryside and listening to the burble of that big, slow-turning engine. *Nick Cedar*

One advantage is that the metal in the lining ensures that the drum will always have a fresh surface, as the linings do tend to turn down the drum a bit after extended use. However, this shouldn't be a problem on a bike used mostly for riding around with one's beloved on the back when the sun is warm and the roads are dry.

In the exhaust department, longer tube mufflers were stuck back behind the rear axle almost to the end of the rear fender. They sat so low that they would drag on any turn taken at more than a gentle lean, and going up driveways the lower part of the muffler would grind.

As for the engine's innards, the oil pump got a new set of drive and driven gears, but other than that the engine stayed the same. Mileage wasn't anything to brag about, 39mpg being the best reported.

Cosmetic changes included the new "AMF Harley-Davidson" long rectangular tank emblem that was to be around until H-D bought itself back in 1981. Now the handlebar switches were encased in one single plastic housing on each handlebar, rather than in the individual metal ones for each switch used prior to this year. Paint continued, to be two-tone with the second color arranged as a split oblong oval starting at the front of the emblem and ending four inches behind.

Next page
The pipes are covered with smooth chrome heat shields to keep the yellow-blue burns from showing. The year 1971 was also the last year for the six-sided tank emblem. *Nick Cedar*

Foot Clutches

Foot clutches and hand shifters were no longer a part of the H-D catalog by 1973, and a good thing that was. By point of illustration, I'd like to relate a small story that took place a number of years ago. The cast is me, a Panhead of uncertain parentage, and the entire city of San Francisco—hills, garbage trucks, and all.

Picture riding a motorcycle with the clutch under your left foot as in a car. It would behoove you to ensure that you get your right foot down for support at stoplights if you roll up in gear, as your left foot has to run the clutch when the light changes. My old Panhead H-D had a foot clutch, without an over-center control to keep it engaged when depressed. That pig was guaranteed to provide the odd thrill now and then. Evidently the bike had served as a sidecar hauler up to the time the owner bought a car, and the clutch had been run as a suicide setup since the old owner didn't have to put his foot down to hold the bike up when riding the side hack. Of course, I got it after the owner had already sold the hack to someone, but it still ran with the suicide clutch, mammoth spring and all. One fine summer's day in my spotted past, when I was young and exploring San Francisco on my prehistoric mount, especially sticks in mind.

I was enjoying the travels up and down the many hills of the city, watching people watch me on my oil-dripping, unmuffled, parts-dropping behemoth, when a light turned red at the top of Franklin Street. And I do mean at the top. Parts of Franklin would rate as a number six ascent in difficulty for free-climbers. Anyway, I found myself up at the top chugging along about 25mph, needing to stop before becoming part of a seafood truck coming from the left. All was fine up to a point. I managed to select first gear before I came to a stop. This saves that little embarrassing moment of indecision while a gear is located when the light goes green and the duck two feet behind you in the sanitation truck drops his clutch with a "clunk" you can hear over your bike's exhaust just before he buries the throttle on his Cummins diesel.

The ol' right foot proudly held up its end on the pavement. Even the front brake was working for a change. If you're keeping track, you see that both feet, and the right hand are fully occupied keeping the bike from rolling back into the garbage scow behind me. The left hand was on light duty, only keeping its side of the bars pointed straight.

One thing I hadn't taken into consideration—Yet! Some of the hills of San Fran are off-cambered for rain runoff. This happened to be one of them. As I sat at what was turning out to be the world's longest light, my bike ever so slowly started to tilt to the left, leaning into the camber of the road. Well, if you've been counting, it was obvious my lower left extremity was fully occupied keeping the clutch in while the right side kept me up. Being the sharp person I was, I quickly realized my options were narrowing at a rapid rate. If I sat there and did nothing, soon I'd be horizontal and a prime candidate to get my neck run over. If I lifted my left foot off the clutch to stabilize the bike, the engine would undoubtedly die, at which time the light would go green and I'd get eaten by 15 tons of garbage on six wheels. If I did what was looking to be my only way out and side-stepped the clutch while punching the throttle, I'd probably end up part of a advertisement on the side of a passing bus.

By this time, I had approached the point of no return as far as lean angle. Figuring it was the least harmful of a number of nasty choices, I wound the throttle to the stop and side-stepped the clutch. All available horsepower thundered to life and the front wheel lofted slightly as the bike launched forward through the red light. The next couple of seconds only took about a month to pass. I know I cleared one car's rear bumper by the thickness of a lottery ticket. I did hear brakes somewhere to my left, but I opted not to look. One housewife type in the crosswalk made a rather rude noise at me in passing. All in all, I figured I got off lucky that time. I also figured it was more than time to part company with that bike, as this wasn't the first time it had enlivened my day with moments of sheer terror. Once it even had the nerve to catch fire, but that was easily dealt with, as there were six of us standing nearby with a good supply of used beer on hand, so to speak.

1973 Electra Glide

Production
FLH 74ci Super Sport: 7,750
FL 74ci: 1,025

Not too many changes took place in 1973, but the ones that did were important. A hydraulic disc brake replaced the hydraulic rear drum. The saddle was made slightly longer, giving a little more room for the passenger. Again, the oil pump was changed, this time with new scavenge gears. The cone gear cover was updated from side oiling to end oiling. The tail lamp, in use since 1955, changed.

The bike now weighed 738lb with the King of the Road package, which included windshield, spotlights, front and rear case guards, fiberglass saddlebags (protected with chrome guards around their sides that tied into the rear case guards), the new sprung saddle, and a half tank of fuel. Wheelbase was 61.4in, the seat put you 34in off the ground—quite high compared to a new Electra Glide Standard with 28in of seat height. Harley rated the engine at 66hp, sufficient to haul all that weight and mass down the quarter-mile at 15.42sec and 84mph.

Cycle World magazine managed to get one to run 0 to 60 in 7.6sec, and they succeeded in bring it back to a halt in just under 170ft. All this and it produced 37mpg.

Now there was no tool box, no centerstand, no kick lever, no lock for the steering head. The turn signals worked as long as you held down the button, a feature carried up through the end of Shovelhead production. Paint schemes were solid color with a transfer decal that consisted of a series of oblong bars 6in by 1/2in carried down the tanks through the center of the emblem.

Harley built a series of 70th Anniversary editions in 1973. In effect they were the same FLH with different trim and paint options. Nice to have if you want a special edition, but only the paint and decals make it different.

Right
Jeff Hackett caught this 1975 FLH one day as it rolled by on a sunny day. Not completely stock, it's still a good example of an older Electra Glide. Check all the chrome covers under the seat. This was so none of that ugly "mechanical" stuff showed from either side. This bike also wears another set of those "quiet" fishtails. Even the exhaust pipes have chrome covers over them to hide any discoloration. I count eleven red lights on the back—how 'bout you? *Jeff Hackett*

A 1973 FLH at speed. I don't know what it is, but Harley ad models always have *such* a satisfied look on their faces. *Harley-Davidson*

1974 Electra Glide

Production
FLH-1200: 5,166
FLHF: 1,535
FL-Police: 900

This year saw the demise of the old Bendix carb, replaced by a Keihin, with fewer knobs and levers to adjust. An alarm system became standard. Mounted in a black box behind the license plate, it was key operated. This is one feature H-D should have kept on all their bikes. The Police model had a Stewart-Warner "Police Special" calibrated speedometer that read from 0 to 120mph and was said to be accurate within 1/2mph.

1975 Electra Glide

Production
FLH-1200: 7,400
FLHF: 1,535
FL-Police: 900

The 1975 model year was pretty much a carryover year. The biggest change was that the old style "spiral" with the control cable inside the right handlebar (in use since 1954) throttle was changed to a modern twist grip with a single-cable external cable with spring return. Also, the ends of the bars sported new grips

Most importantly, 1975 was the last year that the FL motor was offered. From here on out, only the higher compression FLH motor was available.

Left
The "AMF Harley-Davidson" emblem shows prominently on the tank. This bike has some optional trim, like the chrome piece running up the back of the front fender and the rail running down its top, and the front bumper that were options in 1975.
Jeff Hackett

Below left
When the FL was ordered as a police bike, it came with a Stewart-Warner speedometer marked "Police Special" and was supposed to be accurate to 2mph. The choke knob mounts right in the top center of the console with the high-beam, neutral, and oil-pressure lights right below.

Below right
The rear fender on this 1976 FL-P is hinged to make tire changing easier. Funny, I thought that's what dealers were for.

1976 Electra Glide

Production
    FLH-1200: 11,891

All Big Twin models were powered by the high-compression FLH motor because the FL motor had been discontinued at the end of 1975 production.

Our nation celebrated its 200th anniversary in 1976. In honor, H-D offered a Bicentennial Edition for the year. All the graphics were decals applied over black metallic paint. The fairing sported the H-D eagle over the bar and shield with a stylized red-white-blue 1976 over the eagle's head. The tanks had a similar decal over and under the AMF H-D emblem; eagle on top and "Made in USA" underneath. On top of the Tour-Pak was a "Liberty Edition" decal.

The 1976 Police model had the same calibrated speedometer as in prior years.

To celebrate the Nation's Bicentennial, Harley issued a special edition called the "Liberty Edition" of the FLH-1200. Paint was Black Metallic, the seat was black also, and decals commemorating the event adorned the fairing, tanks, and top bag. *Harley-Davidson*

Most specials and limited editions really don't command a premium price on the used Shovelhead market yet. If I were looking for a Harley to put in the front room and watch appreciate, I'd probably look for a 1976 Liberty Edition in the condition that this one's owner, Robert McCollum, has maintained. The decals on the fairing, tour box, and tanks are just about perfect. He's kept the mileage down to 5,200, with the only changes over almost 20 years being the brake calipers. *Robert McCollum*

This "Liberty Edition" decal on the rear trunk was one of the special paint and decals that differentiate the bike from a stock Electra Glide. *Robert McCollum*

1977 Electra Glide

Production
    FLH-1200: 8,691
    FLHS -1200: 535

The transmission received the bulk of the changes for this year. The new main drive gear got new caged bearings; the countershaft got new caged needle bearings. The oil breather valve was improved for better scavenging from the gear cases and crankcase.

The seat now grew a bit longer and was called a "Dual-Bucket." The seat now had a step to it with grab handles on the passenger end. For once the passenger had a dedicated place to sit.

The Liberty Edition's factory paint is a silver micro-sequined flake laid over black. In the sun it looks about nine feet deep. Pictures don't do justice to the paint, as what looks like dust on the Tour-Pak is actually the silver flake. The bike would have to be kept inside, though, or the decals would disappear and the paint fade. This one's for show, not for go. *Robert McCollum*

The Liberty's tank received extra decals above and below the H-D emblem. *Robert McCollum*

The FLHS was listed for sale for the first time, and the new model was the FLH minus the fairing and bags, with just a windshield installed.

1978 Electra Glide

Production
  FLH-1200 74ci Electra Glide: 4,761
  FLH-1200 Anniversary 74ci Electra Glide: 2,120
  FLH-80 80ci Electra Glide: 2,525
  FLH-Anniversary 80ci Electra Glide: 8

This was the year of the big changes. A larger engine was introduced—80ci. Emission control had now reached the point where performance began to suffer badly. Trying to make the V-twin engine conform to ever-tightening regulations concerning noise and what came out the tailpipe cost H-D a lot of performance. There are only two ways to get back what is lost through govern-ment regulation of emissions—either use better technology or make the thing bigger. Harley elected to go for the sophisticated approach of the "If it don't go, make it bigger" school of design engineering. Thus the 80ci engine was born.

Harley hung the new engine in almost every model while still keeping the old 74c version available at the same time. There was an FLH-1200 offered along with an FLH-80.

To make the larger motor, both the bore and stroke grew. The 74ci's dimensions are 3.43in bore by 3.96in stroke pushing out 66 pre-smog horse-power through the early 1970s. On the 80ci engine the bore was opened to 3.50in and the stroke pushed to 4.25in for an actual displace-ment of 81.6ci, but that would have looked a bit awkward on the air cleaner, so H-D called it 80ci. Besides, who wants to say they ride an eighty-one point six-incher? Eighty-incher rolls off the tongue much better.

Harley was never bashful about identifying their bikes. When you rode this 1977 FLH, it proclaimed you were King of the Highway, in case you had any identity problems. It was better than your own personal shrink—still is, for that matter. The saddlebag even had the optional rail across the top cover, making it easy to hook bungee cords when tying down tents and sleeping bags.

Harley-Davidson buyers had lots of options available in 1977. These "fishtails" are all show and no go. The round exhaust pipe can be seen inside.

In 1978, Harley celebrated its 75th anniversary with this special edition Electra Glide. Trim is a bit different, and on the front fender, a gold stripe says "Harley-Davidson's 75th Anniversary 1200cc Electra Glide." *Harley-Davidson*

Factory-stated power, for whatever it's worth, stayed the same as the early 74s, right at 66. The new FLH-80 took advantage of updated engineering and was more thrifty at 49mpg, where as the 1971 Electra Glide did well to pull 36mpg. Performance changed, though. Top speed of the new bike was 89 thundering miles per hour—six slower than the older bike. Oh well, if you wanted speed, there was always the Japanese rice grinders. Mostly the reason for the bigger 80ci motor was to try and retain the performance the smog monsters were eating every year. Visual aspects of the engine only differed slightly.

Cylinders had nine fins, one less fin than the 74ci motor's cylinders.

Mid-year changes in the engines included steel valve guides replaced by cast iron to help eliminate valve sticking (due to leaner jetting), new valves with hardened stems for the same reason, and a new intake manifold with a single lip at the cylinder head that mated to new flat O-rings for better seal than the old round O-rings provided. The ignition went to an electronic "breakerless" type. A new cam gear replaced the old one, in use since 1970.

Sidecars were available in most model years, though not many bikes were ordered as such. This is one of about 300 1978 FL-Ps and FLHs that came stock with a sidecar. Actually, very few FLs came with a hack because the extra power of the FLH was needed to pull the greater weight. *Ken Bradford*

All the sidecar bikes, like this 1978 FL-P owned by Ken Bradford, had a steering damper and adjustable-rake forks installed as standard equipment. Crank down on this knob, and the steering got stiffer, which aided the handling. *Ken Bradford*

Mechanical Ignition

Up until this time, all H-D ignition systems used the mechanical point system to fire the plugs at the proper time. From 1966 to 1977, all the Shovelheads used the same bits and pieces either mounted on an ignition timer sticking up from the right side of the cases, or inside a timing case on the right side of the engine under a cover secured by two screws. Either way, what was inside was pretty much the same: a set of mechanical contact points, a condenser, and a two-lobed cam that is driven off the engine, with lobes that lifted and broke the electrical contact between the movable contact point and the stationary contact point. This break in electrical flow allowed a short pulse of DC voltage to be fed to the ignition coil's low-voltage primary windings. These windings in turn caused a voltage to be generated in the high, or secondary, windings. Just 12 volts went in from the points to the coil, but 6,000 volts came out the other side of the coil through the high-tension leads to the spark plugs. If all was right in the world and the fuel-air mixture was in the cylinders when the spark lit, power was made by the burning gases expanding against the piston, which then transferred the energy down to the crank where it was converted into rotational energy and from there drove the rear wheel by way of a primary chain, gearbox, rear drive chain, and rear sprocket. The whole power transfer to the rear wheels was turned on and off by the clutch.

As the timing cam rotated and lifted the points, two things happened over a period of time causing the timing to shift ever so slightly. The actual contact between the contact point cam follower and the timing cam was a small non-metallic block. As the lobes turned past this block, it slowly wore down, causing the points to close up from their proper .018in gap. If not maintained, the points could close up to where they ceased to break contact and no spark was produced. This was the cause of a lot of hard-starting engines in the past.

Secondly, every time the points opened, a spark was generated between the points. Usually when troubleshooting an engine that refused to start, the mechanic would remove the points cover, turn on the ignition, and break the points contact with a screwdriver. When he said; "Yup, you got spark to the points," this is the spark he was talking about.

Well, every time the spark arced from one point to the other, a small amount of metal was oxidized or burnt. After so many openings and closings of the points, usually around 5,000mi of operation, the points were burned badly enough to hinder electrical contact. This made for a weak spark and poor starting.

Combine the two, points closing up and burnt contacts, and all the bike would do was provide you with a lot of exercise by way of the kickstarter. Or, if you had an electric foot, it would cheerfully turn over until the battery's tongue was hanging out. Back in the 1960s and 1970s a lot of people didn't understand the relative simplicity of the points system and tended to do what most people do when they don't understand something—they left it alone. After a while, the bike slowly started getting harder to fire, especially on those cold mornings when you were a little late to work.

The scenario then sometimes went like this. A call was made to another bike owner who had been riding a few years longer than you, so should presumably know more about what's going on in the electrics department. Just because he only rides a Triumph is no reason to think he doesn't understand what makes a Harley tick. He agrees to come over and bail you out of your quandary—masculine ego won't let him say he doesn't know any more about Harleys than where to put the gas.

Later in the day, he arrives, and the two of you immediately start working on the problem by pulling the float bowl off the carb. Then the float needle falls out of the carb when both of you are playing with the little screw that drains the float bowl—you know, the one you didn't remove before pulling the bowl and spilling gas on your pants. Good thing you left your cigarettes outside.

Then, finding nothing in the float bowl other than some gunk in the bottom, you reinstall it, only stripping one screw in the process. When the gas is turned on and begins to run out the breather onto your already saturated pants leg, you think the float's stuck, so you deliver a healthy blow to the float bowl with the back of a hammer. All this does is spray more gas over the ground. Shut the petcock off, sit and think for a while.

Your guardian angel must be smiling on you today 'cause your buddy rests his hand on the ground, sticking the float needle into his palm. Many hours later, the carb is back to where it was before you started pulling parts. Your buddy says let's check spark. Good idea. You pull one plug lead, insert a screwdriver into the cap and hold it next to the case to see if there's a spark when the engine turns over.

Would have worked better if you had made sure the bike was in neutral before turning the engine over. Oh well, the bleeding will stop eventually and you won't need those fingers on your clutch hand for a few weeks 'cause the bike doesn't run anyway.

This time you ensure the trans is in neutral before trying to turn the engine again. Sure would be easier if you had pulled the spark plugs first, wouldn't it? Now you have it right, plugs out, screwdriver next to the coil, finger touching the metal shaft of the screwdriver. Funny how a spark that makes you jump hard enough to hit your head on the bars isn't enough to light a plug.

Next, the points cover comes off. Now you have a chance to play with all that strange stuff in there.

Anyway, you get the idea. Mechanical devices that rub on each other and wear, coupled with a lack of knowledge about what makes an engine run, will either keep you from riding your bike, or help you obtain an education the hard way. By the way, all the above actually happened over the last 30 years to me, or people I know.

Getting rid of the points for a sealed "black box" ignition system was one of the best things H-D ever did. The basic concept is the same as mechanical ignition, just nothing rubs and wears. The ignition cam now has a trigger in it that causes a signal to be sent when it passes by a sensor. In turn the sensor sends the signal to an amplifier where it's pumped up and sent to the ignition coil where the high voltage is produced in the same way as before.

Even though you hear words like "Hall Effect," transducer, CD Ignition, and others, all the theory is the same; a trigger sends a signal, the signal is boosted, and the coil is triggered. As long as the electronics don't fail, nothing much goes wrong. No arms to break, no wires to short, no points to burn. Usually any electronics failure will happen in the first one or two hours of operation. If you make it through that period, you can be pretty sure everything will work for a long time.

There are a few people going around saying that converting back to mechanical points gives better ignition, hotter spark, finer control of events, or some hooey like that. Mostly they mean they don't understand electronics because they can't see it move, so they want to go back to the old ways. Believe me, if the old mechanical system had any good characteristics, it would be in use today. I don't know about you, but I haven't seen any Indy car mechanics, or the guys who make H-D's VR1000 engine run, with points files or feeler gauges in their hands. Matter of fact, the VR1000 has Weber Electronic Fuel Injection (EFI) tied together with electronic ignition, so both the sparks and fuel mixture are entirely controlled by computer. These days, any tuning or setup requires a lap-top computer as much as a good set of tools.

Don't be surprised to see more of this type of setup appearing on street bikes in the real near future. Harley's new Ultra Classic Electra Glide for 1995 comes with Sequential Port Fuel Injection. Cold starts are no problem, fuel mileage improves, and there's nothing to wear out—at least not in the first 100,000mi.

This seems like a long way to go just to talk about points versus black boxes, but I wouldn't spend the time if I hadn't seen a lot of new (less than 10 years) riders with heads full of old war stories about how "them new 'tronic ignitions ain't worth a pound of used beer. Stick with points, Sonny; at least they can be worked on." Sure can—every 5,000mi, or sooner—whether you want to or not!

Maintenance on the 80ci motor stayed the same as on the earlier engines. Oil changes still covered the pipes with black goo due to the placement of the oil tank drain right above and inboard of the pipes. The usual solution for this is to buy a quick-drain replacement for the oil plug and install it at the first change. It screws into the oil tank just like the drain plug and is set up to be able to fit a plastic hose on the end. Presto—no more spilled oil.

Even back in the 1980s, people were going for the "retro" look. Jeff Hackett caught this 1980 Electra Glide sidecar rig masquerading as a 1950s Panhead. As said before, driving (and you do drive it) a sidecar rig takes a little more work than running a solo rig. First time you try to lean into a corner and nothing happens will definitely make you think. The hard part is getting use to having to point the bars where you want to go. The first few rides are usually quite interesting. *Jeff Hackett*

This year marked the introduction of the FLH 75th Anniversary Edition Electra Glide. Almost all had the 74ci motor. They came with black paint with gold pinstriping on the tanks and fenders and a cast gold eagle on the clutch cover. A leather seat was standard. The front fender had an emblem on its lower rear edge—"Harley-Davidson 75th Anniversary 1200cc Electra Glide."

Seldom mentioned is that eight of the FLH-80 Anniversary bikes were also built in 1978. Other

In 1979, the FLT was born—only 19 were built in that year compared to 4,480 in 1980, so it might be properly said that it came out for real in 1980. Built on a completely new frame, it had a three-point elastomer isolation system for the engine, which drives through a five-speed transmission. The swingarm had repositioned shocks, and the passenger pegs had moved off it onto the frame. An integrated, frame-mounted fairing held two headlights, while a new instrument cluster sat on the tank. The seat was frame mounted and had a large backrest for the passenger. The Tour-Pak and bags came standard. At the time, it was a tour bike second to none. *Ron Hussey*

The 80ci engine in the FLT was free to shake in its mounts. Vibration could be felt up to 2000rpm when the mount's dampening effect came into play. At a stoplight, the engine would shake around while the rest of the bike stood still, but on the road, the vibration was kept to a minimum. This isn't to say the FLT didn't vibrate, just that the vibration that came through let you know there was a motorcycle under you. *Ron Hussey*

than the emblems, the bikes were the same FLH-80s available to everyone in 1978. A total of 2,341 FLH-1200 Anniversary models were built compared to the small number of 80ci Anniversary Editions, so I would think the 80ci Anniversary model might be a little more desirable than its smaller brother. Although, as said before, don't really expect the special editions, differing only in paint or decals, to be worth any more than the regular model of that year.

That's why I advise that if you're looking for an old classic Shovel to ride on sunny Sundays—just you and your significant other enjoying the smog—go for whatever you want. But if you are looking for a scoot that won't require a lot of maintenance in the electrical department, and you like Shovelheads, find one manufactured after 1977, with electronic ignition, and check to see all the stuff in the sparks department is stock.

A new air cleaner grew off the carburetor. In order to help satisfy EPA noise laws, intake noise had to be toned down a bit. The new silencer was approximately the size of a toaster and the nickname stuck. It was also one of the first items to go up on the shelf when the bike rolled into the garage, as the cleaner was too wide for a leg to

bend around comfortably. The size of the engine was imprinted on the flat surface of the air cleaner's chrome cover—"1200" or "80" as the case might be. Cast aluminum wheels were also available on the FLH for the first time.

1979 Electra Glide

Production
    FLT Tour Glide 80ci: 19
    FLHC Classic 80ci: 4,368
    FLHC 80ci with sidecar: 353
    FLH-80: 3,429
    FLH-1200: 2,612
    FLH-80 Police: 84
    FLH-1200 Police: 596

Two new models showed up at this time, the FLT Tour Glide (H-D figures list only 19 built in 1979, probably for pre-intro testing, so it is unclear whether the FLT was officially introduced in 1979 or in 1980) and the FLHC Electra Glide Classic, both powered by the bigger engine, although an FLHC with sidecar was offered and one brochure showed it with a 74ci engine—pretty rare beast, though. The only 1979 sidecar rig I

Smog Motors—the Beginning

Around the early 1970s, the pollution-control storm troopers discovered motorcycles. They already had the cars emasculated to the point where a mid- to late-1970s Pontiac Trans-Am, stuffed full of 455ci and backed up with a four-speed, would run just about hard enough to pull the skin off a chocolate pudding. What had been 450 dirty ol' horsepower in the earlier Pontiacs was now down to somewhere in the neighborhood of 195 very tiny ponies.

Harley also had to dance to the EPA's tune and start cleaning up their engines. Increasing smog laws would finally drive them to build an 80ci engine for 1978 in order to comply with ever-tightening regulations while still providing adequate power to haul the touring bikes around with the same performance as in prior years.

For the first part of the 1970s, H-D was able to get by with stop-gap measures like bigger, quieter air filters and quieter pipes—although the noise difference between the 1972 and 1977 is truly hard to hear. The air cleaner took on bread-box proportions, and the pipes became heavier, packed with much more sound-deadening material. Some said this made the mufflers tend to last longer as there was more to wear out when they grounded on corners.

Slowly, the bikes gained weight and lost performance. By 1973, an Electra Glide FLH, with half a tank of fuel, tipped the scales at 742lb. Now, the bike took 7.6sec to reach 60mph and had a quarter-mile trap speed of 84mph. This put the bike right up in the class of a well-tuned Yamaha 500 single. Not quite as fast, mind you, but right in the ballpark, which was one more reason to bump the engine to a larger displacement. Harley never has tried to

stand out in the performance market with the FL series; however, the 74 was getting so loaded down with noise-reducing parts and smog adjustments that customers were becoming quite fed up with the lack of acceleration. This, coupled with the quality problems, helped drive sales into the toilet.

In all fairness to AMF, the 1982 "Rubber Glides" and the newer Tour Glide had been in the works while AMF was around. Part of H-D's sales drop was due to a worldwide recession, part due to other manufacturers building big touring bikes that didn't break, shake, or leak. Not all the blame for lack of sales can be laid at AMF's corporate door.

Honda popped up with their answer to 700mi days and 700lb loads with their GL-1000 Gold Wing. A basic "Wing" was sold for slightly under $3,000. This was $231 cheaper than H-D's smallest American bike, the Sportster. Also, the Honda folks knew their marketing and had done their homework well. The Gold Wing came backed up by a huge accessory market, ready to supply everything from foot boards to fairings for a price considerably under Harley's.

Plus, in the performance area, the Wing was a rocket ship compared to the FLH. Elapsed time in the quarter-mile for the Honda was 13.13sec, while the FLH couldn't get under 14.6. Even the Sportster, H-D's answer to performance for many years, ran 14.22sec in the quarter. To give you an idea as to how bad the performance was strangled on the Harley, just pulling off the mufflers on the Sportster dropped the ET to 13.30sec—that's a bunch of gain for only a removal of excessive back pressure, but it shows what H-D and AMF were being forced to do to sell bikes while complying with government regulations.

ever saw was an 80-incher and common sense indicates that's the only way they rolled out from the factory. Why would someone opt for the increased weight of a sidehack, only to specify that the smaller engine be installed?

The FLHC Classic had a special tan and creme paint scheme with a brown leather seat, along with the full King of the Highway touring equipment (including Tour-Pak) and cast wheels. The

seats on all FLH models were now mounted onto the frame, making the seat height much lower. The sprung seat could still be had as an option. The FLHC was also offered with a CLE sidecar option. The sidecar had its own brakes operated off the rear brake pedal, and the bike's gearing was lowered to aid in hauling around the increased weight.

1980 Electra Glide and Tour Glide

Production
>FLT Tour Glide 80ci: 4,480
>FLHC Electra Glide Classic 80ci: 2,480
>FLHC with sidecar 80ci: 463
>FLH-80 Electra Glide 80ci: 1,625
>FLH-1200 Electra Glide 74ci: 1,111
>FLHS Electra Glide Sport 80ci: 914
>FLH-80 Police 80ci: 391
>FLH-1200 Police: 528

This was the year the FLT Tour Glide officially hit the streets. The Tour Glide had an all-new rectangular steel backbone frame, three-point elastomer (similar to rubber) isolating engine mounting system. The swingarm had the shocks repositioned so that the lower shock mount is much nearer to the rear axle, reducing swingarm flex and resulting in greatly improved handling. The down side of the new shock position is that they somewhat intruded into the saddlebags, reducing usable space. The passenger pegs moved from the swingarm to the frame. The final drive chain now ran in a fully enclosed oil bath. This was a successful attempt to lengthen chain life while the belt-drive system for the new five-speed Big Twins was being hammered out.

Now, the oil filter followed automotive practice and was a spin-on. The exhaust system was of a rather interesting design. The front header twists around the front of the engine and over the primary to connect to the left muffler. The rear-cylinder header runs forward looping around the timing cover to feed the right muffler.

Standard Tour-Pak and saddlebags hung on back, but the fairing was completely different from the FLH's. It was designed to be more wind-cheating and mounted to the frame instead of the bars as on the FLH. The new fairing also housed twin headlamps, rather than the FLH fairing's single headlight. The FLT's steering head was redesigned to position the forks behind the steering stem, so they worked in trail, and gave lighter steering as a primary benefit. The new steering head also left a lot of room to mount a full fairing.

The FLT frame set the engine slightly higher for better ground clearance, and the new forks and shocks allowed more wheel travel. The new FLT primary cover ties the transmission to the engine and the swingarm pivots on this, allowing the whole assembly to be isolated from the rest of the bike and rider. Further isolating the rider and passenger from the shake, rattle, and roll was the use of better isolation material for the floor boards and bars. The vibration was still there, just isolated. At a stoplight the front wheel would shake in time with the engine, but once the tach rose above 2000rpm, the mounts came into their efficiency range and felt vibration went away. It looked a little strange to see the engine doing its version of St. Vitus' Dance between your legs while the bike motored on serenely (well, as serenely as a Harley ever gets) down the superslab. If you watch another Harley when the rider nails it, the engine actually can be seen to move in the frame.

When the fork tubes were positioned behind the triple clamps, their angle of rake was changed at the same time. This enabled the bike to be moved around at low speed without the need of a forklift. If you ever see a Tour Glide without its fairing, you'll be able to easily spot the differences between it and the front end on an FLH-series scoot.

The bike rode on 16in cast-aluminum rims mounting whitewall tires. Twin disc brakes on the front complemented the single disc on the rear (the solid-mount FLH series never got twin front discs). The transmission was all new, with five gears in place of four. Fifth gear still was a 1:1 ratio, but the other four were a little closer, with first being lower than in the four-speed. Shifting up went "snick." Shifting down still went "KLUNK." Neutral still could only be found from first.

The only engine available in the FLT was the 80ci. Oil fed from a new tank on the right side, with the filler right below the center of the seat. The battery hid behind the left saddlebag, which had to be pulled to remove the battery. The new engine came with H-D's V-fire electronic ignition, and no kickstarter was fitted, nor was there any place to fit one.

The tank transfer went Art Deco—as on the 1936–39 Knucklehead with stylized wings flowing back around the metal AMF H-D bar emblem that overlaid the transfer. The bottom of the front fender had a chrome guard marked "FLT" on both sides, and the ubiquitous air cleaner had a bold "80" embossed in the middle, as on all the 80-inchers.

Two color schemes, charcoal and black or tan and creme were offered, but I saw a bike back in 1981 that the customer swore was stock paint, and it was root beer brown. The factory was beginning to offer custom paint around that time, so that could be how this one came along.

The whole FLT was designed with the American tourer in mind. Speeds above 100mph are largely rhetorical in this country of 65mph limits, so multitudes of horsepower creating 0–60 times under 5sec and 150mph top ends are fairly useless. Lower maintenance and lots of room to haul everything from a spare helmet to m' lady's curling irons are high priorities for the long-distance rider, thus enclosed chain drive to extend chain life—later to go to belt with the Evo—and large empty saddlebags and top box to ensure that nothing got left behind. Smoothness with comfort was the idea. No longer would your arms be totally numb after a two-hour ride. Your feet even stayed on the foot boards when the revs climbed. Parts didn't crack. The bike actually was a pleasure to ride for long distances.

The old saddle used on previous FLHs, mounted on a post and spring setup, was not used because the new frame wouldn't allow the post mounting. To me, the old post mount never felt all that secure in a turn anyway, especially if the locating bolts on the seat were anywhere near worn, so the new seat was welcome. The old seat would give every turn a two-part feeling. First, the bike would lean into the turn, then the seat slid over just a bit with a mild jerk, and your upper body slid over to follow, but there was a slight lag between turning the bike and the seat giving over, depending on age and condition of equipment. You always knew it was going to pop; you just didn't know when.

As usual with new models, the weight went up a bit. Claimed dry weight was 725lb. A 1981 FLT that I saw on trucker's scales went a little over 800lb with a light load on board.

Getting accustomed to the handling of the Tour Glide takes some time. It initially feels like the bars aren't sending signals directly to the front wheel, or the road surface is slightly slick; however, a few miles in the saddle quickly removes any fears of the bike going its own way. The seat is kind of a toss-up for comfort. if you're the type of rider that climbs aboard and sits in the same posi-

tion all day, it'll work for you. Some of us, myself included, like to move around on a seat as we ride. This one has such a cut to the front half that sliding back is almost impossible. You're pretty much committed to one position. At least you can move your feet around to the passenger pegs, foot boards, and an accessory set of highway pegs usually mounted on the crash bars (oops, I mean "over-center restraints").

The bike can be ordered with a Comfort Flex seat option, and this would be high on the list of things to look for when buying an FLT Shovelhead. The seat can be adjusted for firmness and spring dampening by an adjuster reached by raising the seat with its release lever mounted under the right side of the seat. The springs can be set to four different positions to accommodate any weight rider. The seat dampening is controlled by a friction arm whose tension can be varied by tightening a nut on the pivot point. Adjustments can be made at gas stops on very long trips, giving a different feel to the seat as the day progresses.

Logging 500mi days is the bike's forte. With its wide 16in wheels, low center of gravity, and 5.75in of trail on the front forks, the FLT will run for miles with the throttle set screw turned in and your hands in your lap. Actually, the bike is rather reluctant to change direction from the on-center position. Body English doesn't have a lot of effect on its chosen path. To cause a change in direction, one must push on the bars with medium effort to upset the linear stability and start a turn.

Even with all the improvements introduced on the FLT, H-D didn't see fit to install a centerstand or supply a set of tools. Not that I look forward to changing a tire on the beast, but it would be nice to know it could be done without resorting to a dealer and some sort of hoist. For one thing, a centerstand would make adjusting the chain easier. The sidestand is the same mechanical marvel it has always been. When extended and weight is put on it, the top of the arm has a pin that fits into a recess, locking the stand from inadvertently folding. Pick the bike off the stand and a spring drops the arm out of the recess and it's ready to retract.

The fuel tank carries a full 5gal, making 200mi stops not a problem. The newer Shovel engines have an improved oil-control kit and better head drains to help slow down oil consumption.

When you laid down the money for the Heritage, you could have your name engraved on a plaque below the ignition switch. Probably not a good idea, unless you plan on being buried astride the bike. The next owner might not be real happy carrying your name around on *his* bike. The 85mph speedometer brings back memories of the government's attempt to slow down vehicles to the mandated (not voted) 55mph federal speed limit. Not being able to tell how fast you were going above 85mph sure would save fuel—wouldn't it? And you think the government always knows what it's doing.

According to the handbook, maintenance is to be done every 1,250mi, but as this is mostly a series of checks, it's not much to worry about. Oil and filter changes come up at 2,500mi intervals, and most Tour Glides won't need more than a possible quart of oil between changes. If the chain oiler is turned off, oil control can be better than 1,000mi to the quart when the engine is new and filled with H-D's recommended light oil—50w. Hot summers call for a slightly heavier oil; in this case 60w will do. In the days of 5w-30 oil going into

car engine capable of running far past 100,000mi, it seems strange to have to run a bike engine on a lubricant that greatly resembles axle grease, but anything lighter in the engine and oil pressure (what little there is) drops on a hot day. Also, the lighter stuff seems to find its way out of the engine with great enthusiasm.

The last FLT I saw on a rack with its cylinders off had 70,000mi on it. It belonged to the wife of a parts manager at an H-D shop in Southern California. She bought it new, and other than a valve job, it had performed just fine until a valve guide dropped out of the head and created a four-part piston. They told me that during the life of the engine, it had never used oil between changes. The owner did say that she dropped the oil every 1,500mi. That might have some bearing on the low consumption.

The FLT also had a few special designs of its own. The speedometer and tachometer resided in a case bolted to the handlebars. The fairing was directly connected to the frame, though, so when the bars were turned the speedo/tach assembly moved but the fairing didn't. This took a bit of time to become accustomed to, especially if you had just come off an Electra Glide with a fork-mounted fairing and the speedometer sitting on the tank where God and Harley-Davidson intended it to be.

Just so you would be sure what you were riding and what particular type of personality should be put forth when riding the new FLT, a quick look down below the gas tank cover at the words "King Of The Road," set into the gas tank, let you know that when you rode this Harley-Davidson, lesser mortals beware!

Harley-Davidson thought they'd introduce a back-to-basics FLH to counterpoint the massive FLT at 781lb. They took a basic FLH, four-speed, frame-mounted seat, hard bags (but no trunk), and wire wheels—called it the FLHS Electra Glide Sport. No windshield was fitted, and it only came with a single muffler on the right side. The old familiar FLHC Classic "dresser" was still available, now in charcoal and black, in addition to tan and creme, for those who wanted to take it all with them.

The Shriners bought 181 FLHP bikes that year. Interestingly, 1980 police models were officially called FLH-80 or FLH-1200 Police, although paperwork shows that the Shriners bought FLHP models. Either way, H-D doesn't have the records or capability to break down the bikes sold to the Shriners by colors.

There is not a lot of information available about the Shrine bikes, as the only difference between the Shrine and police models is the equipment used for law enforcement duty such as the lights and sirens, with the exception of both getting the calibrated speedometer. The only difference between the standard Electra Glide and the Police models (including the Shrine models), other than the police gear, is the paint, usually birch white, off-white, or white/tan. The bikes intended for sidecar use, be it Shrine, police, or civilian, all had an adjustable front end.

1981 Electra Glide and Tour Glide

Production
    FLTC Tour Glide Classic: 1,157
    FLT Tour Glide: 1,636
    FLHC Electra Glide Classic: 1,472
    FLHC Electra Glide Classic with sidecar: 152
    FLH Electra Glide: 2,131
    FLHs Electra Glide Sport: 1,062
    FLH Electra Glide Heritage: 784
    FLH-Police: 402

This was the end of the 74ci motor. All 1981 bikes were powered by the 80ci with "V-Fire II" ignition. In the engine department, the lower end got a new crankpin, sprocket shaft, and pinion shaft at the middle of the model year. The compression ratio dropped from 8:1 to 7.4:1 to reduce pinging with what passed for gas in those days. As a result, the engine would run on just about anything that would pour through a straw and burn.

Valve guides and seals were elongated to further reduce valve sticking and oil consumption; to further reduce oil consumption, additional drain lines were added to the rocker boxes to reduce the possibility of oil filling the boxes and being forced through the guides.

The Heritage model appeared this year. This bike took the retro look another step backward. It was a basic FLH mounted with a windshield, black sprung seat with grab handle in back and fringes and buckles around the bottom, and sported fringed leather saddlebags—for once deserving their name. They were held closed with three leather straps. Paint was an olive green with orange panels and stripes. Spoke wheels reappeared, and two mufflers took care of the exhaust. No top bag was installed on the rear rack. The only personal identification was a plaque below the ignition switch that said: "This

This 1981 Heritage isn't intended to be a collector's piece. The bike shows 20,000mi of highway wear and tear. The medallion on the clutch cover indicates this is an 80ci bike. Between this and the writing below the ignition switch, it's possible to mistake this as a 1980 bike instead of an 80ci 1981 model. This particular bike is one of the quietest running Shovelheads around. The pistons don't slap, the lifters can't be heard, and the exhaust is particularly subdued.

Another 1980s bike retro'd back to an earlier age. This time, the owner elected to make his 1981 FLH Classic sidecar rig look like a 1963 Panhead. Covering the disc brake to make it look like a drum is a nice touch. The stash pouch behind the windshield is another. *Jeff Hackett*

In 1981, H-D built 784 Heritage Edition FLHs. The bike's colors are the same the factory used extensively up to the 1930s. Olive drab and red sound like a strange combination, but it works on the bike. A Heritage wouldn't be a Heritage without fringe on the saddlebags. Harley has continued to ride the nostalgia wave down to the present day with the Heritage Softail Classic, but the 1981 Heritage was the first.

80 Heritage Edition built for"—and there was a space underneath to have a name engraved. Most owners don't put anything permanent there as the next buyer might not have exactly the same name. The clutch "derby" cover had the Heritage Edition logo with a red "80" above and a set of gold wings below. The speedometer was now the federally mandated 85mph in white numerals with an inner km/h (kilometer per hour) scale in blue.

The '81 FLT got a more conventional exhaust system. The front header bends right and sweeps back to the right muffler, while the rear pipe splits, one branch to the left muffler and the other crossing over to the right header and muffler (well, H-D thought it was simpler).

The FLTC Tour Glide Classic—for those who had everything, but needed more—was introduced, carrying a larger Tour-Pak on back and a

slightly different two-tone paint scheme with a little more chrome trim for emphasis.

1982 Electra Glide and Tour Glide

Production
    FLT Tour Glide: 1,196
    FLTC Tour Classic: 833
    FLH-80: 1,491
    FLHC Electra Glide Classic: 1,284
    FLHC with sidecar: 95
    FLHF Electra Glide Heritage: 313
    FLHS Electra Glide Sport: 948
    FLHP-80 Police: 317
    FLHP-80: 1,261
    FLHP Deluxe: 270
    FLHP Shrine: 19
    FLHP: 282

Not a whole lot was changed this year. The FLT grew a higher output alternator to handle extras like electric vests, additional lights, trailers with auxiliary lights, electric washer and drier—you get the drift. The foot boards became adjustable, the bars changed, and better seals and locks were introduced for the Tour-Pak and bags. Prior to this change, a good rainstorm and 50mph could fill a saddlebag on a long run; a much better seal eliminated this problem.

Down amongst the machinery, the valves and valve springs were updated. Last, but by no means least, there were new plastic switches riding on the handlebars.

Curiously, H-D production lists show that five FLHP models were available: the FLHP-80 Police, FLHP-80, FLHP Deluxe, FLHP Shrine, and plain FLHP.

1983 Electra Glide and Tour Glide

Production
  FLT Tour Glide: 566
  FLTC Tour Glide Classic: 475
  FLTC with sidecar: 37
  FLH-80 Electra Glide (belt drive): 1,272
  FLHT Electra Glide (rubber-mounted engine):
    1,426
  FLHTC Electra Glide Classic (rubber-mounted
    engine): 1,304
  FLHTC with sidecar: 75
  FLHS Electra Glide Sport: 985
  FLHP Police Standard: 334
  FLHP Deluxe (birch white): 414
  FLHTP (rubber-mounted engine; chain drive):
    341
  FLHP Shrine (belt drive): 11
  FLHP (belt drive): 112

Model year 1983 saw the introduction of a new and successful series: the FLHT and FLHTC. Cannily recognizing that many riders wanted the FLT's rubber-mounted engine and five-speed transmission but were put off by the FLT's styling, H-D combined the FLT's frame, five-speed transmission, and saddlebags with the FLH's classic fork-mounted fairing, creating a new ultimate touring bike with classic form and modern function. Now there were two separate and distinct Electra Glide lines: the classic FLH with solid-mounted engine and four-speed transmission and the new FLHT with rubber-mounted engine and five-speed transmission.

If there's a "C" after the model, as in FLHTC and FLTC, that indicates a bigger trunk on back, spiffy paint, and a few chrome touches for the "Classic" look.

To further the never-ending quest for lower seat heights for their advertising copywriters to brag about, H-D gave the FLT and FLTC shorter, stiffer suspension and a cut-down seat. Even the old-fashioned FLH series was given a modern touch: all got the final drive belt as first used on the Sturgis; The FLT and FLHT series retained the enclosed chain.

1984 Electra Glide and Tour Glide

Busy sorting out the last bugs on their new Evolution motor, H-D didn't spend any time updating the Shovelhead motor for its final production run. The last Shovelhead rolled out the factory doors in June 1984, but H-D did see fit to release a few special editions of the Shovelhead FLH and FX models for the 1984 model year. The FLHX last-edition Electra Glide, with full touring gear and fork-mounted fairing, sporting white paint with gold stripes and red pinstriping and wore wire wheels.

The FLHS Electra Glide Sport collected a few Wide Glide parts. Some were built with staggered duals, higher handlebars, forward foot pegs, and controls. Early-production FLHS bikes had the standard setup of dual exhaust and floor boards. Sometime during the middle of the model year, H-D swapped over. Both bikes were wire wheels.

The factory says 467 FLHT bikes were built—232 black and 235 white. A friend of mine in Phoenix has a black one (serial number 1HD1AEK33EY017520—built November 30, 1983) with foot boards and dual turnout mufflers that the factory says was produced halfway through the model run, number 232. His bike has a massive eagle decal on the front of his fairing that he swears came from the factory. The rest of the cosmetics are stock, red and gold striping on the bags and front fender. He thinks, and I tend to agree, this is the last black FLHT Shovelhead built.

Was the 1984 FLT or FLHT ever built with an Evo motor? Two men whose opinions I respect greatly, differ as to the answer; I'll leave it up to

The 1984 FLHS was the last of the FL Shovelheads. By this point, AMF and all the problems with quality were long gone. Now, you could count on the bike actually taking you on a 2,000mi trip without using any oil, or having any of the pieces drop off. This bike has lived in Arizona all its life and spends most of its time inside. The sun would have eaten up the decal on the fairing and faded the paint by now if its owner, Phil Bellini, hadn't kept it under wraps. If you want the bike to stay stock, you pretty much have to give up on the idea of running up lots of miles. *Phil Bellini*

you to find one and send me a picture, care of the publisher.

Harley-Davidson model and production figures do not separate the 1984 production into Shovelhead bikes and Evo bikes. They do, however, list two sets of figures for most models, and one could easily infer that the first set is for production with the Shovelhead motor and that the second for Evolution-powered bikes. I'll go out on that limb and present these figures for what they are worth. These figures show that H-D built in 1984 the following Shovelhead-powered bikes: 446 FLTC, 11 FLTC with sidecars, 974 FLHTC, 14 FLHTC with sidecars, 155 FLH-80 (plus 1,828 Evo-powered FLH-80s, which makes no sense since the FLH supposedly died with the Shovel motor), 791 FLHX (plus 467 Evo-powered FLHX, which again makes no sense), 499 FLHS, 100 FLHTP, and 36 FLHT Shrine. Again, these figures are not exact, but are the best available.

Note that Harley-Davidson figures list several hundred FLH and FLHX models built in 1985, suggesting that Shovels may have been made in 1985. Despite this, the accepted view is that the Shovel, and the FLH, died in 1984.

And so, in 1984, ended almost two decades of Shovelhead touring bikes. What had started out in the mid-1960s as two models—the FL and FLH—that were not all that different from their predecessor, the Panhead, ended up in its last year of production with nine different models ranging in type from the original FLH to the FLHTC.

Many improvements took the 1984 touring bike a long way from the first FLH. Each year from 1966 saw a better bike in the marketplace. Harley was able to improve its bikes and grow as a company even while fighting problems with quality, antiquated equipment, and ownership by a conglomerate only marginally interested in actual motorcycles. If you believe that being "forged in the fires of tribulation" makes for a stronger person, then the same could be said about a motorcycle company owned and operated by extremely dedicated people.

The last full dresser Shovelhead from Harley-Davidson, the FLHTC can only be best appreciated for what it is by spending a few thousand miles traveling across the country on what some say was the last of the "real" Harleys.

PART TWO

The 1971—84 FX Series

As 1970 rolled around, H-D found itself with two products heading in two entirely different directions. The FL series had grown into 800lb road behemoths, suitable for eating miles on the superslab, but not the most maneuverable vehicle once the city streets were reached. The other end of the scale, the Sportster, was trying to be all things to all people. The XLCH version of the Sportster was trying to run in the same performance league as the Universal Japanese Motorcycle (UJM)—usually an in-line four-cylinder with a lot more performance than the Sportster—and the XLH Sportster was being promoted as a small version of a touring bike with its larger tank and optional windshield and saddlebags. This really wasn't where it belonged, but H-D was trying to fill all the niches.

Customs, or "Choppers"

The name "chopper" actually connoted a full dresser that had all the extraneous parts removed down to a light, single-seat, fenderless bike. The old method of how to build a chopper was to start the engine and begin removing parts 'till the bike quit running, then bolt that last part back on.

In later years, the name became synonymous with extended forks, tall "ape-hanger" bars, loud pipes, peanut tanks, and the rest of the modifications that resulted in a bike similar to what was appearing in the wave of 1960s biker movies, produced with casts of tens and costs of hundreds. In reality, all "chopper" originally meant was a clean, fast bike built to run.

Toward the end of the 1960s, choppers began to be popular. Used Big Twins were being stripped of all the extraneous parts unnecessary for function—no case guards, chopped-off rear fender, bobbed or no front fender, and lose the big seat. A healthy coat of some basic color—black being predominate—and a set of loud pipes (punched-out factory mufflers would do if the wallet wouldn't handle any custom work) completed the bike.

Ensuring the rider could be seen, a set of high bars raised him up enough to have to lean back in the saddle and hang his feet on highway pegs, mounted in front of where the foot boards used to be. Now he was set to profile down main street.

Just to prove that not everyone was sleeping at H-D during the AMF years, the stylists at H-D, typified by Willie G. Davidson, grandson of one of the founders and now head of design and styling, went to work to build a factory version of the chopper that anyone could, and hopefully would, walk into the dealership and buy.

Reaching into the parts bin, they picked out the front fork assembly of the Sportster, along with its front wheel and brake. This was mated to a stripped FLH frame and 74ci engine. The whole collection of parts weighed in at 559lb, about 50lb over a Sporty.

The 1971 Super Glide had a massive taillight parked in the middle of the white fiberglass seat. From some angles, this being one of them, the bike had a fairly strange look.

1971 FX-1200

Production
    FX Super Glide: 4,700

Thus was born the FX Super Glide. The "F" came from the FLH, whose motor and frame were used; the "X" from the XL Sportster that contributed the front end. The FL frame sprouted a few new tabs to mount the new equipment, such as those for the new brake pedal and linkage. The FLH's foot boards were replaced on the Super Glide by conventional foot pegs. The left peg mounted to a lug on the chain inspection cover on the primary case (where the FLH's passenger peg mounted), and the right peg mounted through a bar that extended forward from a clamp on the engine-trans locating plate to put the peg in line with the left one.

Instead of designing a new shifter linkage to accommodate the new, more rearward left foot position, H-D engineers merely reversed the shift

Here's where all the factory custom Harleys started. In 1971, H-D grafted the front end of a Sportster to the frame of an FLH. A lot of unnecessary weight was pared off, like the electric starter, dual exhaust, and saddlebags. The only controls on the buckhorn bars are the two turn-signal buttons and the high-beam switch. No electric foot, no stereo—just basic bike. Harley planted a large "1" decal on the tank, so no one would have any trouble with model identification, or where the bike fit in the scheme of things. Red, white, and blue were the only colors for America's "#1 Freedom Machine." The English went slightly potty over this bike. It was written up in every British bike rag available, and everyone who even got to sit on it wanted one worse than breathing. The plastic rear fender/seat combo was only around for one year and is now quite a collector's item. *Marty Greersen—Harley Davidson*

lever on its shaft so that it was reachable by the toes of the left foot on the new peg. Of course, reversing the lever also meant reversing the shift pattern: On the first FXs, first was up and the other three gears were down. This could really screw you up if you owned an FLH and an FX. Or it could prove to be real interesting if you were used to a different bike like a Honda with the standard shift pattern. Fortunately, after a few years, the factory designed a linkage just for the FX, on which the shifter shaft inserted through a hole in the primary case, putting the shift lever behind the peg and giving the bike a standard shift pattern.

Finding neutral in most of the Shovel gearboxes can be a bit of a problem. With the engine off, the bike will have to be rolled slightly while

The emblem on the 1971 Super Glide tank stood out from a red and blue border. The AMF decal has drifted down towards the bottom of the 3.5gal twin tanks (optional on the FLH). *Ron Hussey*

The gearshift lever on the 1971 Super Glide had been turned around to put it closer to the pedal, resulting in a reversed shift pattern: one up and three down. This owner has spun his shifter 180deg so the pattern is back to the standard one down and the rest up. The bolt head should be on top of the lever where it attaches to the shaft, not the nut. *Ron Hussey*

stirring the lever. If the engine's running, it's near impossible to go from second gear to neutral. My standard procedure is to drop into first while still rolling up to a stop, then lift the lever halfway up and hope the trans pops into neutral. This is somewhat of an art and needs to be practiced for a while before you become proficient at hitting neutral instead of second gear.

The brake master cylinder stayed where it had always been on the FLH, but H-D engineers designed a new linkage to connect it to the rear-mounted rear brake cylinder. The pedal attached to the same mounting point as the right foot peg, then swung under the front exhaust pipe and up to put the pedal in front of the peg and slightly higher, where it was easily reached.

No electric starter was fitted, allowing the smaller battery off the Sportster to be installed on the right side, up high, almost under the seat. The kick lever was fitted with a slim, rounded pedal instead of the wide, flat one on the FLH. Passenger foot pegs mounted on the lower shock mounts because the normal mounts now had the rider's pegs.

The optional 3.5gal twin tanks for the FLH were mounted, and the speedometer, warning lights, choke, and ignition switch were located in the same chrome center console used on the FLH. A black insert behind the console filled in the

This FX has the shifter mounted in the proper position. *Marty Greerson*

space between the tanks and in front of the seat; a large red-white-blue "1" was prominently displayed in its center. The top of the "1" was blue with seven stars in two rows, the vertical riser had vertical red and white stripes, and the bottom had the company's name on a white background. The horn and its chrome cover—two additional parts borrowed from the Sportster—mounted on the left front downtube.

The FX's exhaust system was all new because the FX's right foot peg position prevented H-D from reusing the standard FLH two-into-one system. The new exhaust consisted of two individual pipes sweeping back from the cylinders welded together in a "Y" just before the single muffler. The rear pipe was routed behind the kickstarter. The muffler was a chrome-plated version of the old tube-type muffler that had been the standard muffler on most 1950s and 1960s Pans and Shovels.

The most striking difference was the seat. Harley had a golf-cart business that was good at making fiberglass bodies and parts for their carts and fairings and sidecar bodies for their bikes. They designed a boat-tailed fiberglass fender/seat combination unlike anything anyone had seen on a Harley before. The taillight tunneled back into the fender almost to the back of the seat. The front of the fender swept down to swingarm level to provide splash protection. This all was attached to the familiar rear fender rails used on the rest of the big bikes.

Fenders and tanks got basic white paint with blue accents above the tank emblem and red below. A small AMF decal rode in the bottom tank accent (many of these must not have had a very good quality of glue as a lot of them seem to have fallen off rather rapidly). Two red stripes ran down the side of the rear fender, and a blue flash tapered from the back of the seat to the top curve of the rear fender. A red center stripe with two blue accent stripes ran the length of the front fender. The air cleaner cover was plain chrome with no adornments.

Stopping power was by full-width drum brake actuated by a lever on the right side of the front wire wheel and the standard rear cast-iron drum on the left with the sprocket mounted on it. The chain guard was chrome plated unlike the black-painted one on the FLH.

The white basic color, with red and blue panels and striping, really made the first Super Glide stand out; even with a factory in the background. *Ron Hussey*

Harley hit upon a good idea with the FX-1200. In its first year of production, over 4,700 were sold. The FLH only outsold it by 775 units. But by 1974, the FX and FXE outsold the FLH by a wide margin.

Now that H-D had regressed back to a kickstarter on the FX Super Glide, the old drill of fuel, choke, throttle, ignition, and kick had to be learned all over. A lot of different methods were put forth by the bike magazines of the day. I think some of them had a lot of fun going through the litany of kickstarting just to prove a Harley is still a Harley.

Most methods went something along the lines of this: turn on the fuel, kick once or twice

with the ignition off and the choke on, then turn off the choke, on with the ignition, and try it for serious. When that didn't work, the *Cycle World* method of three kicks with full choke and then ignition on when cold, or one kick—no choke— when hot, seemed to bring the motor to life with fair regularity. If none of these methods worked, it still looked good in your front room, didn't it?

When the bike was finally urged to life, and if your right foot would still support you enough to climb on the bike, you could count on performance significantly better than that of the standard FLH. Zero to sixty times were down to 5.6sec—a vast improvement. The quarter-mile

This blue Super Glide shows its Sportster front end quite clearly, right down to the drum brake. The two-into-one pipe actually worked better than the factory duals, producing a bit more power. The engine was still advertised with the same 66hp as the FLH. *Jeff Hackett*

passed by in 14.43sec, close enough to give a Sportster a good go.

A few very brave magazine crazies from *Road Rider* said the bike was very stable at 120mph, but how they urged it to that velocity is beyond me. The only way I know to get an FX up to 120 per, is to make a sharp right turn in the middle of the Golden Gate Bridge and check the speedometer just prior to hitting the water. Top end was more like 105mph—reached after a long run with a small rider. That's OK, though. Most of us were content just to get the bloody thing started from cold and go enjoy a ride on a much lighter big Harley.

1972 FX Super Glide

Production
    FX Super Glide: 6,500

Except for cosmetic details, the second-year FX was the same as the first. The boat-tailed rear fender on the 1971 FX wasn't popular, so for 1972 the FX went to an XL-style fender with a different seat, and the boat-tails went to the trash can—much to restorers' dismay because they are quite valuable today.

For the new FX fender, a set of new alloy rear frame rails had to be fabricated to fit. A standard banana seat sat on top. The six-sided emblem went away, to be replaced by a rectangular version with "AMF" proceeding "Harley-Davidson." Other than that, the FX stayed the same. The motor was still rated at 66hp, and torque—what really made the bike pull—still was 70lb-ft at 4000rpm. The red, white, and blue paint scheme gave way to H-D's standard single color with accents around the tank emblem.

The rear master brake cylinder was repositioned below and behind the right foot peg so that it was actuated through a shorter linkage. The pedal no longer had to snake underneath and around the outside of the front exhaust pipe because the pivot was now above the foot peg instead of below.

The restyled FX was an even bigger hit than the original had been. Production increased to 6,500 units, exactly 1,800 more than for the previous year.

1973 FX Super Glide

Production
    FX Super Glide: 7,625

The 1973 Super Glide received many changes. Starting at the front, Japanese Kayaba forks with orange reflectors on the lower tubes and a single disc brake replaced the straight legs and drum of old. The rear brake was also changed to a disc. The tank was completely different; now a single 3.5gal unit mounted up on the frame with more space between the bottom of the tank and the top of the engine. Personal opinion of the author: this has to be the ugliest, dorkiest tank ever built by H-D. The new tank looked very similar to the ones on H-D's Italian-built 350cc Sprint (the tank looked ugly there too). The tank was painted in a solid color with narrow rectangular bars circumnavigating it with the gas cap and emblem interrupting their passage. Willie G.

Normally, the kickstarter lever return spring has a cover over it, as shown here. That way, if it breaks, it won't do any damage should it depart in little pieces. If this does happen without a cover installed, don't worry; your leg will keep all the chunks of spring from falling on the ground.

The 1971 FX came with a plastic rear fender over the FL frame. Harley only used it for one year, then went to a conventional type. The one on this bike sports a trick paint job, but otherwise is the same shape as when it came from the factory. Due to their rarity, these fenders are becoming quite valuable.

must've let this one slip by. Just to prove this was no aberration, the same paint scheme found its way to the FLH with similar resulting appearance. Because the new tank lacked the former tank's center console, on which the speedometer was mounted, the 1973 FX's speedometer was mounted to the handlebars behind the triple clamps where it was driven off the front wheel; still no tach yet.

The ignition switch changed to a small round housing below the left side of the tank. The choke sat right below. The fuel on-off lever was 2in behind the ignition. New plastic switch housings (same as those introduced on the 1972 FL) replaced the individual metal switches formerly used. A hydraulic master brake cylinder sat on the right bar and actuated the front brake through a new lever.

One positive styling change was the switch from the two-into-one exhaust to a set of classic staggered shorty dual exhaust pipes with no crossover pipe—similar to those on the XLCH.

Several other minor changes were also evident, such as that the passenger pegs were repositioned from the lower shock mount to the forward part of the swingarm.

Despite the new tank, Super Glide sales increased again in 1973, to 7,625, a mere 125 bikes fewer than FLH sales that year—maybe

because many Super Glide buyers looked on their new mounts as raw material for their own custom machine, so they were not put off by the "bread-loaf" between the seat and the bars.

1974 FX and FXE Super Glides

Production
    FX Super Glide: 3,034
    FXE Super Glide: 6,199

FXE Super Glide

A new Super Glide model was introduced for 1974, the electric-start FXE. The FXE was identical to the FX, except that it had an electric starter and the slightly larger battery from the electric-start XLH Sportster. The new electric foot made it easier for those who didn't have the forbearance and strength of a Ugandan mountain gorilla. Now, getting the Big Twin to life was a simple matter of a little choke and a little button. Sales also showed that a lot of people wanted the chopper image, but didn't want to have to work at it.

Harley was slowly making the Super Glide its own machine with its own parts and linkages distinct from those used on the FLH. In 1972, the FX had gotten its own master cylinder; in 1974, it got its own new shifter mechanism. As part of the new mechanism, both Super Glide models got a new chain inspection cover with a revised left foot peg mount and hole for a new shifter shaft that operated through a new linkage. The shifter now pivoted behind the peg, passed up and over, and operated in the conventional "one-down, three-up" manner. The inner primary cover had to be changed to accommodate the shifter shaft passing through to the shifter linkage.

Carburetion now was controlled by a conventional twist-grip throttle and a single sheathed cable routed outside the tube of the handlebar, instead of by the 1954-style "spiral" with its control wire hidden inside the handlebar tube. The free turning throttle of old was gone, a victim of federal regulations that insisted the throttle be self-closing. A return spring enabled the throttle plate to snap shut if the throttle was released. In order to provide the cruise control similar to the older style throttle, a jam screw was fitted underneath the throttle grip housing. By screwing in the tensioning screw, enough pressure could be exerted

The first 1971 FX Super Glide came with Sportster front forks and triple clamps, mounting a drum brake, an Electra Glide frame, and a fiberglass rear seat. It was painted in patriotic colors and in England was called the "Sparkling America." The British really took to it, and it was featured in Warr's, the oldest motorcycle shop in Britain. The English riders wanted it bad, but it cost the equivalent of a year's salary for most. It was the first of all the Harley semi-customs.

against the twist grip to keep the throttle from closing. The FLH series got the new throttle in 1975.

The transmission got a higher first gear on both bikes, requiring a new mainshaft and countershaft.

The tank stayed the same as in 1973—this time with a set of stripes running under the emblem from its front edge to the rear of the tank and over the emblem in a different color, running from the rear of the emblem to the front of the tank. More factory options like trident-forked sissy bars appear. The list of optional semi-chopper parts grew . Turn signals appeared on the bars for the first time. And a tach joined the speedometer in a new nacelle.

Judging by the number of sales—electric start made the Super Glide attractive to a much wider audience, and for the first time, Super Glide sales outpaced Electra Glide sales.

1975 FX and FXE Super Glides

Production
   FX Super Glide: 3,060
   FXE Super Glide: 9,350

The 1975 FX and FXE models were essentially unchanged from the 1974 models.

Super Glide sales continued to rise, to 3,060 for the FX and 9,350 for the FXE. In fact, FXE sales alone for 1975 were higher than combined sales for the 1974 FX and FXE. Super Glide sales rose higher every year, and sales of the FXE accounted for all the increase.

1976 FX and FXE Super Glides

Production
   FX Super Glide: 3,034
   FXE Super Glide: 13,838

The 1976 FX and FXE were similar to the 1975 and 1974. Only small changes appeared during these years. Exhaust systems varied from staggered duals to Siamese headers joined below the cylinders and rolling back to one muffler; then staggered duals again, this time with a balance tube between them.

Liberty Edition

The United States' Bicentennial was being celebrated in a big way, and not to be left out, H-D

In 1972, the fiberglass rear fender gave way to an XL style supporting a frame-mounted seat. Minus the sissy bar (a dealer option), Larry Orton's 1974 FX could pass for stock. Most owners lost the AMF decal about as fast as they got the bike home and in the garage. This one looks just about perfect; the whole bike shows like new. In 1974, the Super Glide was available for the first time with an electric foot. This FX came kick-only. *Larry Orton*

came out with a Liberty Edition of the Super Glide. Basic color was Black Metal Flake. The tank had a decal—well it was almost all decal on the top—starting with a gold-and-white scroll around the filler neck. A gold H-D eagle with upswept wings framed the scrollwork. Below the bird was the "Harley-Davidson Motor Cycles" bar and shield in gold, and the balance of the tank carried another scroll with "1776" on one wing and "1976" on the other. "America" was prominently displayed at the base of the scroll. All in all a lot of decal. Unfortunately it was also prone to fade and crack like all other decals, and if you find one in good condition, try to keep it out of the sun as much as possible. The side emblem got the gold-scroll-and-flag treatment also. The coil cover acquired a gold cast eagle, joined by another one on the headlight mounting nut chrome button cover.

If I owned a Liberty Edition—be it FX or FLH—I'd spend some time looking through *Hemmings* or touring flea markets trying to acquire another set of decals, at least for the tank, and fairing in the case of the FLH. Gas tanks for these years aren't real expensive, so I would probably keep the original tucked away and run the spare. Black Metal-flake paint is easy to do, but trying to hand paint those decals, if a replacement set is unavailable, would be a major undertaking.

Super Glide sales accelerated to 3,857 for the FX and 13,838 FXE. The sales dominance of the Super Glide models had reached the point where 1976 FXE models alone outsold FLH models.

1977 Super Glides and Low Riders

Production
    FX Super Glide: 2,049
    FXE Super Glide: 9,460
    FXS Low Rider: 3,742

FXS Low Rider

Late in 1977, the FXS Low Rider appeared. I consider it one of the best looking of the Super Glide series, and wouldn't mind one in my garage. I don't know what I'd use to pay for it, but I'd still like one.

It only came with Gunmetal Gray paint with large red "Harley-Davidson" transfer in two lines of block letters. The dual, 3.5gal tanks (from the

In 1973, Harley hung on the frame probably the ugliest fuel tank ever made. This 1974 FX still carried the tank. The fuel on-off petcock attached to the bottom left, behind the ignition, of the FX's "breadloaf" tank. *Larry Orton*

original FX Super Glide) reappeared with speedometer and tach mounted in the middle on a new console, subsequently used on all Low Riders and later Fat Bobs and Sturgis models. Cast-aluminum wheels built by Morris replaced spoked wheels—19in in the front, 16in in the rear; the edges of the rims were polished. Dual discs rode up front, and a single disc mounted on the right side in the rear.

A new Showa fork replaced the Kayaba. The frame was raked (steering head kicked out to a shallower angle) to stretch the wheelbase and drop the front of the bike. Shorter, stiffer, rear shocks lowered the rear. All this coupled with a thinner stepped seat lowered the seat height to 27.4 in; hence the name.

Flat drag bars on rolled-back risers crowned the forks. Below, the engine cases, barrels, and heads had a black crackle treatment with polished cooling fins, although the cone gear cover and primary cover stayed bare aluminum.

Highway pegs sat in front of the main pegs. An oil cooler rode between and above them, standard for the first time. The exhaust system went to two separate pipes running back to separate attachments on a rather large single muffler with a slight flare and semi-slash at its opening.

The Low Rider was stable in a straight line, but the ride became rough and unsettling when pressed into a corner. Mileage ran near 47mpg, and with sufficient room it could be urged to at

The shifter had been brought through the primary case and the pattern had changed to give the standard one-down, three-up shifting, but the tank wouldn't change up through the end of Shovelhead production. Production figures show 3,034 FXs and 6,199 FXEs built in 1974; by 1983, only 1,215 FXEs were built. *Larry Orton*

least a screaming, mind-blowing, speed-of-light 98mph. This was complemented by a blistering 15sec quarter-mile. Perhaps the 625lb running weight had something to do with its lackadaisical performance. The crouched, low, muscular profile of the Low Rider projected a new image.

FX and FXE Super Glides

Meanwhile, the FXE came with staggered duals, minus the crossover pipe, and shared a new tucked-in kickstarter (the pivot to swing out the pedal was moved to the bottom) with the FXS. From 1977 on, the Super Glide was the budget Big Twin, plainer and cheaper than the Low Rider; this would continue until its discontinuation. It still carried the ugliest tank in motorcycledom, and as the newer, fancier models appeared, the Super Glide began to look even more plain. It could be had with an optional cast rear wheel, though.

The new FXS Low Rider sold 3,742 copies despite its late introduction. These sales came at the expense of some FX and FXE sales, which dropped to 2,049 and 9,400, respectively.

1978 Super Glides and Low Riders

Production
FX Super Glide: 1,774
FXE Super Glide: 8,314
FXS Low Rider: 9,787

Changes were minimal for the FX series in 1978. The Low Rider lost its drag bars for a set of pull-backs. It was also available with optional silver paint with black tank panels and red decal. The "AMF" shrunk, and the factory's logo grew. Both fenders received a black stripe with red pin-striping.

Due to noise regulations, the air cleaner grew to the point where clearance and room for your right leg on the peg was a problem. Usually, when the bike arrived at its new home, the air can was the first thing to go, with the stock pipes following closely behind. The 80ci motor appeared in mid-year, identified by a large "80" on the air cleaner (74s got a "1200"), but weren't available for the FX series until the next year.

In only its second year of production, the FXS outsold the FXE by over 1,400 units, 9,787 for the FXS and 8,314 for the FXE. The plain, kickstart-only FX languished even further in sales, at only 1,774 units sold, so it was discontinued at the end of 1978.

1979 Super Glides, Low Riders, and Fat Bobs

Production
FXE Super Glide: 3,117
FXS-1200 Low Rider: 3,827
FXS-80 Low Rider: 9,433
FXEF-1200 Fat Bob: 4,678
FXEF-80 Fat Bob: 5,264

Once H-D found out that factory customs sell faster than beer at a baseball game, there was no stopping them. In 1979 the FX line was the best selling of all H-D's production. Lots of new things happened in that year. The FX series grew to include the Fat Bob, a Low Rider with different paint, buckhorn bars, one-piece king-and-queen seat, and optional wire wheels.

The Fat Bob and Low Rider could be ordered in 74ci or 80ci persuasion. The FXE (the FX was discontinued) came only with the 74ci motor.

The FXE picked up another front disc and a Siamesed exhaust system. The Low Rider gained a sissy bar and a stash pouch. The meaning of the word "stash" back in 1979 may have had a different meaning than it does today. The connotation was that all FXS riders were bad dudes and carried their drugs, drug paraphernalia, and other "stash" of questionable legality in a small pouch perched under the headlight where it would be the first place searched by an officer of the law—another case of trying for the "look" without really walking the walk. Sure sold bikes, though.

Riders wanted the new 80ci motor. The 80ci

Low Riders and Fat Bobs outsold their 1200cc brethren by large margins: 9,433 FXS-80s compared to 3,827 FXS-1200s, and 5,264 FXEF-80s compared to 4,678 FXEF-1200s. With its wire wheels, ugly tank, and unraked frame, the increasingly plain-looking FXE Super Glides suffered on the showroom when parked near its fancy siblings, and FXE sales dropped to 3,117, less than half the previous year's total.

1980 FX Series

Production
FXE-1200 Super Glide: 3,169
FXWG Wide Glide: 6,045
FXS-1200 Low Rider: 3
FXS-80 Low Rider: 5,922
FXB Sturgis: 1,470
FXEF Fat Bob: 4,773

FXWG Wide Glide

The introduction of the 1980 FXWG heralded another year of big changes for H-D's FX line. The Wide Glide was a factory chopper taken to its limits. Start at the front forks—a set of stripped and stretched forks set wide apart (like those on the FLH) and the 21in spoked front wheel. A smaller headlight fit between the stanchions and sat above a very abbreviated front fender.

Black 5gal dual tanks held a set of red-to-yellow flames igniting at the front of the tank, curling around the gold bar-and-shield logo and burning to fine points halfway down the tanks. The rest of the paint came in any color requested (black, real black). The black was carried onto the engine and cases with fins polished, but the rocker boxes were polished, and the standard chrome air cleaner cover was used. A speedometer from the FLH now resided in the middle of the tanks; no tach was offered.

The seat now split into two sections, the rear rolling up onto a sissy bar. New, forward controls unique to the Wide Glide (at least for 1980) set the rider's feet way out front—standard position foot pegs were gone. In the 1980 sales brochure, H-D called them "highway pegs," but seeing as how there were no other rider's pegs, the term "forward controls" is more appropriate.

Back at the rear, the fender was bobbed and valanced. The stop light was carried under the rear valance, up out of sight. The staggered dual pipes carried a blacked-out crossover pipe running beneath the massive air cleaner.

All these modifications were a culmination of ideas that started right after World War II and were given a massive boost in 1969 by Peter Fonda as Captain America in the movie *Easy Rider*. He rode a Panhead built on a custom frame with a peanut gas tank of about 6oz capacity, painted up like an American flag. The front end was out so far it was almost in the next frame, and it mounted a 21in wheel on a spool. This bike probably did more for the custom chopper scene than any other bike built before or since. Today, the bike comes across ludicrous, with its rigid frame and zero front brakes, but believe me, after this movie made its

run through the drive-in theaters of middle America, everybody who ever thought he wanted to ride a bike and be an imitation hard guy, wanted a bike like Peter's. In less than a year, its clones and copies sprung up all over, and to a great extent, they're still selling—witness the 1980 H-D Wide Glide.

For 1980, you could get all the looks of Fonda's bike without all the discomfort that came with riding it. The FXWG was a factory purpose-built chopper aimed at the crowd who wanted the lean, mean look without having to build it from scratch, or endure the thumps and bounces that came with riding a hardtail (no rear suspension) frame. The Harley "Softail" is a design that tucks the rear suspension underneath and looks

The 1977 FX came with staggered duals (not the ones in the picture, but similar, without crossover pipe.), and all models of the FX got a new kickstarter lever with the pivot at the bottom instead of the top. The Super Glide would remain the entry-level big bike, plainer and cheaper than the new-for-1977 Low Rider. This bike's seen a tank and wheel change, and the rear disc has been drilled. It shows how far an owner will go to change his bike to what he wants, not what the factory builds.

Probably one of the most beautiful Shovelheads, the 1977 Low Rider projected an image of the hard-core biker. It was built for looks rather than performance, and it succeeded; 3,742 built in 1977; 9,787 in 1978, and a total of 13,260 of both engine size, 74ci and 80ci, in 1979. In 1980, the preference for the 80ci motor was shown with three FXSs with the 74ci motors built compared to 5,922 FXS-80s. *Ron Hussey*

like a hardtail. The Softail frame came along in 1984).

The Wide Glide came by that name from its fork tubes being spaced wider apart than those on the other Super Glides. Early choppers would sometimes leave the stock FLH wide steering head on the front when they mounted the 21in wheel. Spacers took up the extra room on the front axle left over from removing the wide 16in wheel and

brake assembly and adding a skinny wheel. This gave the effect of the front wheel sitting all by itself way out there on the end of the forks.

In the Wide Glide, H-D built its own version of the same thing, only with twin disc brakes to aid in hauling the thing down to a stop. The boys who built the original spool front ends found they needed to leave a lot of space between their front wheel and whatever was going down the road in front of them because, although the rear brake did in fact stop the rear wheel from turning, it had little effect on forward motion. This led to a few nasty incidents of bent front ends, sometimes with extensive repairs required to the rider as well.

The Wide Glide fulfilled its purpose of looking good; it wasn't, however, the most comfortable place to be on a 200mi ride. The combination of the high bars making your arms fly like the sails on an America's Cup contender and the reclined seating position setting all your weight on your lower spine, ensured that you were more than ready to get off the thing after an hour or so of looking good. For a cruiser rolling to the local watering hole, it couldn't be beat. Going on a trip—take something else, unless you're under 25 and have a very high tolerance for pain. Ride one for 10 years, and I guarantee you'll be on first-name basis with a chiropractor.

All of the bad points mentioned above didn't do much to retard sales of the bike. A total of 6,045 Wide Glides went out the doors in 1980—5,166 in 1981. Willie G. and his design partner Lou Netz had hit upon a winner. With its staggered duals and "high-in-the-front" stance, partly brought about by installing shorter rear shocks to complement the longer front end, it announced that the owner was a little different from the average rider. Ironically, the desire to be a little different from the average led Wide Glide riders to be part of a large crowd, for in its first year of production, the Wide Glide became H-D's best-selling model.

The first-year production Low Rider came, in 1977, with separate pipes into a common muffler, low flat bars, and a seat height 2.5in lower than a Super Glide's. The Low Rider was 70lb heavier than the kickstart-only FX model of the Super Glide. The tach and speedo were mounted on a new console between the 3.5gal tanks. A 19in front and 16in rear Morris cast-aluminum wheel came standard. The frame was raked to stretch the wheelbase and lower the front new Showa forks. The back dropped down courtesy of shorter shocks. Paint was a gunmetal silver with red H-D decals on the tanks. The crankcases, barrels, and cylinder heads were black, although the cone cover and primary cover were left aluminum.

FXB Sturgis

In 1980, H-D was in the chopper/custom bike business in an even bigger way. If you had a bad desire for a set of flames on the tank of your scoot, H-D was there to oblige. Just belly up to the bar at your local dealership and order an FXWG to go—hold the pickles. You got a bike that the factory had built with all the bits and pieces hung on it that you were going to do just as soon as you rode the thing home and got next week's paycheck. This was the epitome of factory participation in building customs, and it showed H-D knew which way to go to reach its customer base.

Next up on H-D's list of factory customs was the FXB Sturgis. It was named after a motorcycle rally called "The Black Hills Classic" held in Sturgis, South Dakota, every August. Sturgis is the rally for Harley-Davidson riders, so it was only natural for H-D to build the Sturgis. It's not a touring bike to ride halfway across the country to South Dakota, but a bike to take to the rally, perhaps behind a motor home, and cruise the scene. Were I to ride to Sturgis on the Sturgis, I might drop the bike off a trailer at some near town, like Bear Butte—eight miles out of Sturgis (really), and ride on in from there.

Spring 1980 saw its introduction. The Sturgis was based on the 80ci Low Rider with lots of blacked-out parts and with primary and rear drive provided by toothed rubber belts, rather than by chains. The trans had to be worked around so the wide (compared to chain) rear belt would fit. Internally, the gear ratios were raised. The same 3.5 gal tanks from the Low Rider appeared with a tach and speedo mounted in the center console. Thanks to the feds again, the speedometer, mounted forward on the tank, read from 0 to 85; the rear-mounted tach covered 0 to 8,000rpm—a figure not many H-D engines were likely to see.

The wheels were cast aluminum with a red pinstripe around the flat part of the rim. Riders got a king-and-queen seat with sissy bar, all similar to those on the Wide Glide. The primary cases, crank cases, cylinders, heads, gear-case cover, rocker boxes, air cleaner, coil cover, transmission, handlebars, and other small parts were either black or blacked-out.

Spark was provided by the new V-Fire electronic ignition giving better starting and overall performance. The kickstarter still remained, though—just in case all the electrics went dead, or the owner wanted to look bad while kicking it to

On the Low Rider, the tach read to 8000rpm and the speedo went to 150mph, but the bike would pull maybe 106mph after a long run, and spinning the engine above 5500rpm was an exercise in noise. The bike sure looked good, though—especially when it was your eyes watching the gauges. *Ron Hussey*

The 1979 Low Rider came with a kickstarter along with the electric foot. It could be had with either the 74ci or 80ci engine up through 1980. If you are looking for something a little different and rather rare, a 1980 FXS-1200 (74ci) would be a good way to go. This 1979 FXS has forward controls, solo seat, and an S&S carb, but is otherwise factory stock. The owner, Richard Meyer, keeps all the stock parts carefully put away.

The kick lever was still there in 1979, but for most it was for appearances only. It added to the look of the FXS Low Rider—helped the image of the sunburned rider with the thousand-mile stare and well-worn right boot.

Harley sold 9,942 FXEF Fat Bobs in 1979—4,678 as 1200s and the rest as 80-inchers. The Fat Bob was a Low Rider with buckhorn bars, different paint, a different seat, and with the option of wire wheels. Most owners opted for cast wheels, making this black bike owned by Steve Liebenau fairly rare. About the only changes to the bike were some extra chrome, yellow plug wires, and mounts for saddlebags.

life. I actually knew a dude who would make a large production out of getting up on the lever and whomping it a good one, all the time while his right thumb depressed the starter button; what can you say?

One thing that will really get you noticed on a Sturgis is the blackness of the bike. Most of the engine, all of the fenders and tank, and the frame is all black. Some red, mainly around the wheel rims, outlines the black enough to draw your attention to just how black the bike is. This is the style and look that Willie G. and H-D were trying to achieve. The bike *will* get you noticed.

With the Sturgis, H-D really came out with a Shovelhead featuring ideas for the future Evolutions. Its major claims to fame were the two

drive belts replacing the primary and final drive chains. Harley had sat down with Gates Industries and redesigned the drive system on their bikes to take cogged belts. This turned out to be more than a bolt-on affair, and for a while almost didn't happen. For equal strength, belts have to be wider than chains. The transmission had to be redesigned for belt clearance, and the starter had to be moved out of the way. Belts don't have master links, making removal a somewhat complicated affair. Service on the primary belt turned out to be a major task. Harley later dropped the primary belt partly for this reason, but was still able to provide a sealed primary case, even with a double-row chain that needed oil, and this went a long way toward eliminating leaks.

This Low Rider is probably one of the very few with the stock air cleaner. If you look hard, you can see the numbers "1200" on the cleaner. Liebenau said the only reason the muffler was changed was that the original had rusted out.

The Fat Bob came with two individual fuel tanks with a tach and speedometer in the middle, just like on the Low Rider. Trying to read these gauges at any rate of speed is somewhat difficult as your eyes have to shift and refocus down low. Also the 150mph speedometer has the numerals so close together, they are hard to read at a glance. This is one case where a 0–120mph speedo would make more sense, as not too many Harleys will ever see the needle over on the far right side.

The belts first met with a lot of resistance, riders being the traditionalists they are. Lots of owners were concerned with belts breaking while on a trip. Motorcycle magazines of the time advocated changing the belt when the rear tire was changed, as new tires usually required different tools than the average rider had at home. Also, a method of lifting the back of the bike far enough to clear the rear tire was necessary, and why not swap the old belt for new at the same time the rear tire got changed? We've learned a lot since then about belts and longevity, but someone had to pioneer the changes.

Harley came out with numerous ads at the time, extolling the virtues of belts over chains.

Among them, lack of oiling made for a cleaner bike and not having to adjust the belt after the first 500 miles made for less maintenance. When compared to a drive-shaft system, H-D said in effect, drive shafts are great, they last forever—hand them down to your kids. Belts took less power to drive and should last at least 20,000mi.

Actual operation shows a life span more like 30,000 to 40,000mi, depending on how the bike is ridden. For the first few years, H-D included a spare "get-home" belt that could be clipped on if the drive belt broke. This proved more a sop to customer worries than an actual necessity and was soon dropped.

The 1980 FXEF Fat Bob let you sit down in the seat and plant both feet firmly on Mother Earth.
Henry Agundez

The Sturgis took advantage of H-D's desire to build custom motorcycles. To follow the chopper look, H-D stretched the front end 2in. The steering head had a 31.4deg rake angle. What that means is that the front forks have more kickout than the standard offering. Draw a line straight up from the ground to the center of the front fork triple clamps. For our purposes, this will be a perpendicular line relative to the ground. The angle made between the front forks and this imaginary line is the steering rake. Most Harleys get by with an angle closer to 28deg. Stepping the front end out to the Sturgis' rake does two things. First, it gives the bike the "look." Second, it makes the bike want to run in a straight line—*really* want to run in

a straight line. As a matter of fact, the increased rake of the Sturgis caused the bike to run the straight and narrow unless a lot of effort on the bars was made to change direction.

The increased rake, coupled with the bike's 64in wheelbase, made it about as stable as a Chevy Suburban. The mildly tuned engine made it just about as fast, too. Nail the throttle, power shift the transmission, hold the throttle to the stop—just a little under 15sec and the quarter-mile flashes by. Well, maybe the word "flashes" isn't quite appropriate. The Sturgis will beat the traffic if pushed, but that's not its real intent.

For down-and-dirty touring, the FXB-80 Sturgis could be set up with a tent and sleeping

This bright red 1980 FXEF Fat Bob shows what most owners do as fairly standard changes. The seat's different, lower to the ground. The engine wears an S&S carb and breathes out through aftermarket pipes, in this case fairly quiet ones.

bag strapped to a sissy bar, or maybe even a set of leather saddlebags hung over the rear seat, and taken out for long tours. Sit back in the breeze, hang your feet on the highway pegs, and enjoy the scenery as the engine spins along at a slow 2700rpm and 60mph. I did it one summer for two months, my wife and I riding individual Harleys—her on her first bike; and my friend Brian riding his just-purchased Sturgis. That time will always live in my mind as the best ride of my life. Three people, three bikes, 200mi per day, and when we stopped

in campgrounds, we drew people out of their motor homes to sit and talk with us.

Most were surprised that one of the riders had her own Harley—a 1978 FLH, if my failing memory serves me right, and all the retirees were amazed at how we rode in, pushed down the sidestand, and in 15min had tents up, a campfire painting us, and something cold in our hands. If you think life gets much better than sitting 'round a fire watching the flames reflect off your brand-new bike while you listened to the river run by—

Either cast wheels or spokes were available on the Fat Bob. Only the 80ci engine was available; the 74ci saw its last in 1979 on the FXEF; 1980 saw 4,773 built. This one belongs to Hank Ortega and has already been down to the frame and back up in restoration. He says it goes every day (remember, this is California, some of these shots were taken in November—it was 77 degrees).

The Fat Bob, with the 80ci engine, continued to be a popular bike. It was straight-forward and clean. Plus it carried enough fuel to really go somewhere and look good when you got there. This 1981 has the cast wheels instead of wires. *Chuck Gerwig*

The 1980 Wide Glide was one of the first factory customs, inspired by the countless modified Harley-Davidsons put together in shops and garages. The factory custom and retro bikes became the rock Harley-Davidson founded its phenonomal success of the late 1980s and 1990s.

The Super Glide and Fat Bob were dubbed as street machines with a touring bike's soul in this brochure. Both featured V-Fire II electronic ignition, 8:1 compression ratios, and single 38mm carburetors. The Superglide had the 74ci engine, while the Fat Bob sported the 80ci version. *Harley-Davidson*

you are reading the wrong book. The three of us rode four states, two national parks, and a multitude of KOAs while America grew older and the leaves began their journey from green to brown. Three Shovels, 3,100mi of mostly empty roads, and not so much as a broken fingernail. I still have the bike, I don't have the wife, but the memories of those days dodging falling leaves will stay with me forever. That's why my bike sits on a rug in a warm garage. It's given more to me than a lot of people…

The FXB Sturgis was a limited-edition bike, of which H-D records show 1,470 having been built.

The Name Game

For those of you trying to keep up with all the FX bike names, here we go. A Super Glide is a sorta stripped down Electra Glide with the XLH Sportster front end, the 3.5gal single tank, and the .07-candlepower Sportster headlight, guaranteed to make riding after dark an interesting experiment in how

much you can't see. This includes that large animal 100ft in front of your 60mph bike. Yes, some things have to suffer for style. The FXS Low Rider is an FXE Super Glide with more goodies hung on it and a better suit of clothes (twin tanks). The FXEF Fat Bob is a Low Rider with slightly different bits. The FXB Sturgis is a Low Rider with belt drive and lots of black. And the Wide Glide is a Low Rider with bigger tanks, the FLH speedo in the center console (no tach), wide and tall front end, 21in front wheel, and forward controls.

All these motorcycles share a few things in common. The same 80ci Shovelhead engine powers them, except on the FXE, which all had the 74ci motor, and on the FXS-1200 models. The same basic frame (although some differ in rake), shocks, brakes, and lights grace all the bikes. Differences are in cosmetics and items like wheels, pipes, seats, and tanks. The Wide Glide probably departs more from the FX mold than does any of the other bikes.

FXE Super Glide, Fat Bob, and Low Rider

Just 10 full years after the first FX was introduced, the FX line had five distinct models and totally dominated H-D's sales. Total FX sales were 21,422 versus 11,992 for the FLH/FLT. The Super Glide remained the entry-level, low-dollar bike in the FX series. All Super Glides for 1980 were built with the 74ci engine. Sales for the model were up slightly, to 3,169. The FXS Low Rider was available with either motor, but the larger motor was the overwhelming choice of buyers: 5,922 FXS-80s were sold compared to just three FX-1200s. The FXEF Fat Bob was only offered with an 80ci motor. Most of the increase in sales for the other models came at the expense of Fat Bob sales. Just 4,773 were sold, down from 9,962 in 1979.

1981 FX Series

Production
    FXE Super Glide: 3,085
    FXWG Wide Glide: 5,166
    FXB Sturgis: 3,543
    FXS Low Rider: 7,223
    FXEF Fat Boy: 3,691

In 1981, H-D decided to quit competing with itself in the engine department. Most of the big bikes had been offered in 1979 and 1980 with both the 74ci and 80ci motors. Real performance differences, and that between the two engines were minimal; the 80-incher had a skosh more

The Low Rider was another factory custom, with the same basic dimensions and 80ci engine as the Fat Bob but were a lower, leaner look; highway pegs; and some additional pinstriping. Harley-Davidson complemented the Low Rider with a tarted-up Sportster dubbed the Roadster. *Harley-Davidson*

By the 1980s, Harley-Davidson had really pushed the edge on paint schemes. These are just two of the factory custom ideas for bikes. *Harley-Davidson*

Below
You even could find a bike already set up with flames on the tank, if that was your desire. In 1980, Harley-Davidson introduced the FXWG Wide Glide. What helped set it apart were the wide, extended forks holding a 21in spoked wheel, black tank with red and yellow flames, and a 16in rear spoked wheel under a bobbed fender that swoops up at the rear and carries the taillight mounted under the valence. Forward-placed controls (not highway pegs) came standard. This lets you ride in the wind with your arms in the air and butt firmly planted in the low seat. Image? You want image? This bike had it in spades (and flames). *Harley-Davidson*

torque to flog the iron down the road was about all. Even so, the 80-inch was priced slightly higher than the 74—must've cost more to make bigger holes in the cylinders?

Come 1981—no more problem—no more 74. From then until now, the only engine size available in the FX- and FL-series bikes was the 80ci, be it Shovelhead or Evolution. And yes, I've heard, you know a guy who has a friend who knows a dude with a 1981 FLH resting in his well-locked garage in another state with a 74ci engine in it. It's a leftover that H-D put together in the few first 1981 bikes. Well, perhaps, but don't try to win much money at the bar over it. Late 1980 with a 74—sure. Leftover 1980 with 74—OK (H-D didn't always sell everything it made each year, believe it or not!). But a 1981 with a 74, well…

FXE Super Glide

For the first time, the FXE came with an 80ci motor (probably only because the 74ci was no

longer made). The kickstarter disappeared. Still, the entry-level big bike, its sales decreased slightly, to 3,085.

FXWG Wide Glide

For 1981, the Wide Glide was little changed, except that the flame paint job was joined by a metallic black scheme with gold pinstripes. Sales declined by about 900 units, to 5,166.

FXB Sturgis

The Sturgis was also updated only slightly. The most important change was from belt primary back to double-roller chain. The most visible change was from flat drag bars to chrome Buckhorn bars. For 1981, the Sturgis was no longer a limited edition, and sales more than doubled, to 3,543.

FXS Low Rider and FXEF Fat Bob

Along with all the others, these models got the new V-Fire II electronic ignition. The Low Rider was the sales star of 1981; sales increased by more than 1,200 units, to 7,223. Fat Bob sales continued their decline, to 3,691 for 1981, so the model was dropped at the end of the year.

1982 FX Series

Production
    FXE Super Glide: 1,617
    FXS Low Rider: 1,816
    FXB Sturgis: 1,833
    FXWG Wide Glide: 2,348

The FX-series lineup was pared to four for 1982 because the FXEF Fat Bob had been dropped. Changes to all rigid-mounted-engine FX bikes were nominal, but the new rubber-mounted FXR series made its debut (see next chapter). The FXB Sturgis got gold cast wheels and black paint with gold pinstripes on the fenders and tank. New plastic switch housings appeared on all FX bikes this year.

Sales for the whole rigid-mounted-engine FX series declined alarmingly because of recession, increased competition from the Japanese, and introduction of the rubber-mounted FXR and FXRS: 1,617 FXE Super Glides, 1,816 FXS Low Riders, 1,833 FXB Sturgises, and 2,348 FXWG Wide Glides were sold, a minor fraction of what

The FXB Sturgis was the first production bike with twin belt drive—primary and rear. The transmission case had to be altered to clear the wider rear belt, and the gear ratios were higher. The primary belt reverted to chain in the 1981 model year. Staggered dual pipes let through the Harley sound. And boy, was it black! Tanks, cases, cylinders, heads, rocker boxes, air cleaner, primary—even the horn was black. It sold 1,470 in 1980; 3,543 in 1981; and 1,833 in 1982 , its last year of production. *Harley-Davidson*

The tachometer on this 1980 Sturgis is red-lined at 5300rpm. The speedometer reads to 150mph. The bike would just break the century mark with a stiff tail wind; the top third of the speedometer was only for show.

Tariff to the Rescue

Something else happened along about the start of the 1980s—bike sales went down the toilet. Motorcycle sales for bikes over 650cc dropped by 35,000 unit, between 1981 and 1982. Harley definitely felt the squeeze when that transpired. People had to be laid off, production backed down, and on-hand inventories were reduced. The Japanese, however, still continued to fill the pipeline with low-cost big bikes until they ran out of warehouse space. Big Japanese motorcycle dealers were selling bikes for $40 over cost, paying their salesmen $15 per bike (salesmen were standing in line for the job: $15 per bike x 5 bikes per day = almost enough money to support a 23-year-old man) and hoping to make their money on dealer holdbacks and rebates. A 1982 Suzuki could be bought for less than $3,500, while H-D had their FXRS priced almost double that figure.

In September 1982, H-D petitioned the International Trade Commission for protection in the way of a tariff on Japanese manufacturers, who H-D accused of dumping bikes here for prices not only less than they could be purchased in other countries, but also less than they cost to build. Thousands of unsold Japanese bikes had built up in dealers' inventories. This accounted for the strange practice of selling hoards of new

1982–85 bikes alongside the identical 1986 models in a lot of Honda, Suzuki, Kawasaki, and Yamaha shops. This also contributed to the sudden death of a lot of dealers during 1986 and 1987 when the market became saturated with Japanese bikes, and garages all over this country were full of 1000cc, 100hp bikes with less than 2,000mi on them. At one point large dealers were selling bikes cheaper than the smaller dealers could buy them from the factory. That most of those dealers are but a dim memory today doesn't do much for the people put out of business when the market collapsed and sales of new units dropped over 50 percent.

On April 1, 1983, President Reagan signed into law a tariff on all Japanese motorcycles above 700cc. The tariff was for five years, slowly declining from 45 percent to 10 percent and ending in April 1988. The Japanese protested, but there was nothing they could do about it other than cut back on their production of large bikes. This gave H-D the breathing room to build back up. Now the only American motorcycle company left sits at the top of the heap, totally dominating all sales for bikes above 750cc. When you see a big bike coming down the road, the odds are it's a Harley.

---

each model had sold at its peak. At the end of the year, the FXS Low Rider and FXB Sturgis were discontinued.

1983 FX Series

Production
  FXE Super Glide: 1,215
  FXWG Wide Glide: 2,873
  FXSB Low Rider: 3,277
  FXDG Disc Glide: 810

FXSB Low Rider

A new Low Rider was cataloged for 1983: the FXSB Low Rider. Not much was really new on the FXSB, however. It was really just the old FXB Low Rider with the rear belt drive of the FXB Sturgis and replaced both those models for 1983. Proving that many riders thought the belt drive a desirable

feature, the new model was the top seller of the FX lineup, at 3,277 units.

FXDG Disc Glide

The Disc Glide was also new for 1983, but it was just a limited-edition Wide Glide with a solid aluminum disc wheel at the rear, a set of black shorty duals, and the belt final drive from the Sturgis. Only 810 Disc Glides were built.

FXE Super Glide and FXWG Wide Glide

Harley engineers were hard at work developing the next-generation engine and new models, so the FXE Super Glide and FXWG Wide Glide models were essentially carryovers from 1982. Sales of the Wide Glide rose by about 500, to 2,873, while sales for the FXE Super Glide fell by about the same amount, to 1,215.

The 1982 FXRS was introduced at York, Pennsylvania, in June of 1981. It had a totally new frame with FLT-type elastomer motor mounts. The seat flipped up to show the battery and oil tank within easy reach. The 80ci motor fed from a new 4.2gal tank with filler hole and fuel gauge in the center. The tach and speedo were borrowed from the Sportster and rode on the bars. Wheels on the FXRS were cast; a cheaper version, the FXR, had wires and came without the padded sissy bar or highway pegs of the upscale bike. This picture shows a pre-production FXRS wearing wire wheels, but all the production models had cast, ten-spoke wheels.
Harley-Davidson

1984 FX Series

Harley-Davidson does not separate models and production between Shovelhead bikes and Evolution bikes in their published production figures. As noted in chapter one, they do, however, list two separate sets of figures for most models (and sometimes more), so I'll go out on the proverbial limb of speculation again and assume that the first set is for Shovelhead-powered bikes,

and the second set is for Evo-powered machines. If so, then H-D built 942 Shovelhead FXSB Low Riders (versus 1,935 Evo) and two Shovelhead FXWG Wide Glides (versus 2,225 Evo) in 1984. Figures for the FXE Super Glide are too confusing to decipher because they include listings for both single-tank and twin-tank models—with two sets of figures for each! Finally, two figures are shown for the completely new model, the FXST Softail, suggesting that 3,303 Softails were built with the Shovelhead motor before the final 2,110 were built with the Evolution motor (some sources insist that all 1984 Softails were powered by Evo motors, but sightings at the time and these figures hint that some were built with Shovelhead motors). The FXST Softail is basically a Wide Glide with a new frame incorporating a new suspension that hid the shock absorbers underneath the engine, giving the bike the look of a hardtail bike.

Having progressed from the kickstart-only 1971 FX to the electric-start, rubber-mounted engine FXRS, the stage was set for the future—a new, state-of-the-art, V2 engine and new models taking advantage of the Softail, culminating in the FXSTSB Bad Boy, ultimate in the "retro" look—springer front end, a rigid-appearing frame, and a cloisonné tank emblem, all hinting at the past, while the ultra-reliable Evo motor insures a trouble-free future.

Park a 1995 Dyna Low Rider next to a 1972 FX Super Glide and the similarities become readily apparent. Chart the changes over the years and see how Harley-Davidson, the company, grew with Harley-Davidson, the motorcycle. The Evolution truly evolved from the Shovelhead.

1982—84 FXR Series

Production
    FXR: 3,065
    FXRS: 3,190

Now that Harley-Davidson had successfully mounted the FLT's engine in rubber and mated it to a five-speed transmission, the company decided to bring out FX-series machines with the same type of mounts and the five-speed. The FLT frame without fairing looked too strange to be used on the FX, so an entirely new frame had to be designed. Harley fired up the computer (no, H-D engineers didn't still use beads sliding on strings) and came up with a frame that both looked good when exposed and enabled the engine to be mounted in isolastic mounts. A Sportster-type front fork and headlight assembly was fitted to the new frame, and the bike was called the FXR and accompanied by the more upscale FXRS.

More than just the frame was new, however. The oil tank was mounted in front of the battery under a flip-up seat. The new 4.2gal fuel tank filled through a single hole in the console on the tank's top, and a fuel gauge mounted forward of the filler.

Originally, the name Super Glide II was hung on the bike, but that lasted only a short time. Other names were tried for a while, among them Sport Glide, Low Glide, and the nickname "Rubber Glide." None of them seemed to take hold, and I mostly just called mine an FXRS.

The only similarities between this bike and all the FXs that had gone before it was the name on the tank. It came with a five-speed transmission hooked up to a Shovelhead engine with many new internal changes. The oil piping system was updated with a new oil-control package. New lines helped return oil from the heads to the crankcase instead of it building up in the heads and being forced past the valve guides. Also, a new valve guide and seal package was part of the improvements. Compression dropped to the 7.4:1 level, making the bike much happier on pump gas. Performance didn't seem to suffer much, if at all, with the 0.6 reduction in the compression ratio, as it was as fast as all the other FX series.

The FXR's frame was a great deal stiffer in torsion than the older tubes used on the FX. This meant that the bike resisted flex much better than the others, making for improved handling in the twisties. The shocks were moved back on the frame, and their lower attachment point was at the end of the swingarm instead of in the middle as before. This gave the swingarm more support and less flex out at the end where the rear axle was mounted. In turn this made for less movement of the rear wheel around the swingarm. If you look at the two in a comparison shot, you can see how the old swingarm was able to apply more force to the mid-mounted shock than the new

FXR swingarm with the shock right above the centerline of the wheel.

The FXR and FLT series were H-D's first serious attempts at vibration control. The engines still shook all the time, only the vibration didn't pass to the rider. Well, that's not quite true either. Below

By suspending the engine in rubber mounts, vibration wasn't allowed to pass through to the rider. The engine in the rigid-mount bikes would try to slide your feet off the pegs or boards above 3500rpm, while the rubber-mount FXRS and FLT smoothed out enough to make long distance a pleasure. If you remove the engine from a Rubber Glide, be careful with the mounting system. Go by the book as far as setup, or the mounts may not function correctly.

On my bike, the exhaust manifold bolts gave me so much trouble that when the unleaded gas conversion was done, I had the exhaust ports re-contoured to take three bolt flanges, as shown in this picture.

2000rpm, the mounts didn't come into effect, so the bike would shake clean out to the end of the bars, and the front wheel would bounce in time with the engine while you were stopped at lights. Brakes on, it vibrated one way. Brakes off, another. It was amusing to watch, and my brother, mounted on a Japanese V-twin, got a kick out of it. He couldn't see how anything built in the late twentieth century could run so rough. He figured that my H-D would be worn out and worthless after about 10,000mi. Fifteen years later, his 1981 Japanese twin is worth maybe $600, while the FXRS will bring over $8,500.

Once the clutch engages and the tach passes 2000rpm, the rubber mounts come into play. They are tuned to absorb almost all of the vibration above this point. Some still reaches your hands, but only enough to let you know you're on a motorcycle, without putting your arms to sleep.

My 1982 FXRS had somewhat of an interesting event connected with the new oil-control sys-

Just to show how far an owner will take a bike, this is a 1982 FXR with a few modifications.
Jeff Hackett

This customized 1982 FXR is far from stock, but a better representation of the Shovelhead-powered Harley-Davidson models seen on the streets. Very few of these models remained in factory condition for long. Exhaust pipes, air-cleaner covers, carburetors, and intake manifolds are all likely candidates to be replaced with aftermarket parts. *Jeff Hackett*

tem. In October 1993 I took it into the local dealer to have the heads pulled and the exhaust ports updated with the three-bolt modification, along with having the unleaded gas conversion done at the same time. The lead mechanic noticed something strange about the front head once it was in his hands. One of the oil-return passages hadn't been drilled when the bike was built. Evidently, whoever had been responsible for punching holes either couldn't count or was asleep when my heads came by.

The shop told me about the problem and also mentioned they had called H-D and informed them about the missing hole. This was in 1993 and the bike was built in November of 1981.

Harley said, "Yeah, go ahead and take care of the problem and submit a warranty form." The shop repeated to them the year of the bike, thinking they hadn't heard right the first time and thought the shop said 1992 instead of 1982. Long pause on the other end, until the factory rep came back and said do it anyway.

"It wasn't right from the factory, so we'll stand behind our product and fix it for the customer."

You might think because I write Harley books that this was a favor, but rest assured, the shop didn't know I was a writer, and the factory didn't know my name, which wouldn't have made any difference at all, as I can well attest. They were just standing behind their product. Wonder if any other company, motorcycle or other, would do that. It went a long way toward making believers out of myself and people I've told about it.

Performance benefited from all the improvements. The bike would never be accused of being a canyon terror, but it held its own with anything other than the plastic rockets, and would leave all the other Harleys for dead on a winding road. It wasn't exactly a stone in a straight line, either. Again I have the road rats at *Cycle World* to thank for the figures. They definitely will wring more performance out of a bike than 99.999 percent of the rest of us. They thrashed an FXRS through the quarter-mile in December 1981. Speed was 91mph, elapsed time was 14.26sec. It ran out of oomph at 105mph, as I can testify. There was more left on the tach; the engine just didn't want to pull any harder.

FXRS

The FXRS came with a few more goodies than the FXR. The engine was painted black, and the fins were polished. It had a sissy bar with back pad factory installed and a couple of other minor cosmetic changes, including two-tone paint and highway pegs. The crankcases (cone case left bare aluminum), cylinders, heads, air box, and exhaust crossover were blacked-out. The wheels were cast, as opposed to wires on the FXR. The seat lifted up to reveal the oil tank and battery as on the FXR. Now adding water to the battery or checking oil became a minor chore, so it got done more often, adding to the bike's reliability.

Due to my job taking me all over the world (literally) during the first few years I owned the bike, I didn't get a chance to put more than 5,000mi on it before 1989. It still had the original battery up till then, and it always lit off on the first compression stroke. However, after it sat unattended for six months in 1990, it finally wouldn't start, and I had to buy a new battery. Poor quality if you ask me. Only eight years of neglect, and the damned battery wouldn't hold a charge. The replacement battery lasted until 1993, and now I'm on my third—none of which were H-D parts.

Touring on the FXRS is a pleasant experience for a bike not intended as a real long-distance hauler. It is comfortable running down the road between 75 and 85mph, though, and 400mi days are actually not bad. I did cheat a bit and install a windshield, which aids immeasurably as my body approaches the 50-year mark. The "wind in the face for hours" stuff is beginning to tell on me. Years back, I rode 1,000mi rallies without a care—now a little six-hour chug from San Jose to Los Angeles has me looking for the Tanqueray and a soft bed.

The bike's definitely up to long hauls, even if I'm not. It consistently returns over 45mpg and uses little oil between changes. Having a set of highway pegs along with the standard ones makes moving around on the bike much easier.

One problem I've encountered of late has to do with the instruments, particularly the tach. About 90 percent of my riding is done with the engine turning below 3000rpm. Now that the bike has a few years on it, the tach has grown so accustomed to running below 3,000 that the needle sticks briefly when I run the engine past that point. The tach drive is totally electrical, eliminating a possible dry cable. I think the lubricant in the bushings inside the gauge has become sticky with age and lack of use, perhaps a cleanup and re-oiling would take care of the problem. I'm a little reluctant to open them up for fear of finding a broken something, because parts for these Japanese gauges are totally unavailable. The speedometer is also beginning to show a slight bit of the same thing. I pulled and cleaned the cable, oiled it with a good cable lube and checked for kinks, but it still sticks—same bushings inside?

I wasn't the only one who jumped on one of the new FXRs. Harley sold 3,065 of the FXR model and 3,190 of the FXRS model, meaning that each of the new models outsold any of the solid-mounted FX models.

1983 FXR Series

Production
    FXR: 1,129
    FXRS: 1,413
    FXRT Sport Glide: 1,485

FXRT

The FXRT Sport Glide was introduced in late 1982 as a 1983 model. It was really just an FXRS with the addition of a frame-mounted fairing, hard saddlebags, and a few other goodies. It had a hard time gaining acceptance with the tradition-

oriented Harley buyers due to its nontraditional look. It had all the usual H-D fixtures, but it was covered with a different-appearing fairing. Called the Sport Glide, it was aimed at the sport-touring market shared by BMW and others.

Rolling down the road on the FXRT was actually quite comfortable. The FXRT's frame-mounted fairing, which showed some wind-tunnel influence, is quite similar to the one on the 1980 Tour Glide. The FXRT was a touring Harley for those who spent most of their time running on two-lane roads. The 1984 FXRP police bike, beloved steed of the California Highway Patrol (CHP), drew a lot of its styling from the FXRT. The one CHP I did see on a FXRP said it was a lot more comfortable than the four-cylinder 1000cc Kawasaki police bikes, but didn't have quite the point and squirt of the Japanese bike. Harley made a good deal with the CHP, and they continued riding Harleys until the price difference got too great and they went back to the Japanese bikes.

The Tour Glide will make a good touring bike for those of you who are looking for something lighter than an Electra Glide for long, state-crossing rides. It also shouldn't set you back as much as some of the other FXR series, due to its different styling and general lack of acceptance on the market. Still, it's a Harley, with rubber engine mounts and, in addition, sports a fairly simple pressurized anti-dive front fork. When the front brakes are applied, an electric valve closes between an air tank and the fork tubes, lessening the total volume of air in the system. When the front end tries to dive, it has to work against the increased pressure in the tubes and that slows down the rate of travel, or dive. Release the brake lever, the valve opens and the front end goes back to a soft ride—neat and simple. The rear shocks were also air-assisted.

The FXRT also came with an enclosed chain, just like the larger FLT series, so that'll help keep the gunk off you on long rides. The hard saddlebags have removable liners, semi-waterproof and easily carried into a motel room. Good way to pack ice and liquid refreshment, too.

A solo rider, looking for a Harley to go places, probably could make a pretty decent deal on a

The all-black 1981 FXB Sturgis shows its low, lean look. *Doug Mitchel*

low mileage FXRT and not lose a penny in depreciation for as long as he, or she, kept the bike. I'd probably buy one for my wife, but since the only way I can communicate with her is through her divorce attorney, I'll skip it for now.

FXR and FXRS

In only their second year of production, sales of the FXR and FXRS each fell by 50 percent or more, to 1,129 for the FXR and to 1,413 for the FXRS. At the end of the year, the plain FXR was dropped from the lineup. The new FXRT did not generate the interest on the showroom floor that H-D had hoped for. By the end of the year, only 1,485 had been sold. Considering that the sales of the Low Rider improved and the Wide Glide climbed 525 units over the year before, it was clear that the customer was voting with his dollars for the chopper look. Overall sales of the FX series for 1983 were down 13 percent, possibly accounting for some of the decline in FXR sales.

1984 FXR Series

The FXR lineup for 1984 included only the FXRS and the FXRT, both of which may have been built in limited numbers with the Shovelhead motor for 1984, before production switched entirely to bikes with the new Evolution motor.

The major change to the series, besides the new motor, was the lowering of the FXRS and naming it the Low Glide. In an effort to reduce the cost of production and lower seat height, H-D gave the FXRS shorter shocks and forks with stiffer springs and eliminated the right front brake disc. While these mods made the FXRS more like a conventional Harley, and saved the company some money, they also ruined the bike's excellent ride and completely changed its sporting nature. Did most Harley riders care? Probably not, because the bike stayed that way in following years, and sales increased, but it is interesting to note that the longer suspenders and extra disc were again available starting in 1985 on the FXRS-Sport. Maybe some riders did care after all.

Harley-Davidson does not separate models and production between Shovelhead bikes and Evolution bikes in their published production figures. As said before, they do, however, list two separate sets of figures for each model, so I'll go out on that limb one final time and assume that the first set is for Shovelhead-powered bikes, and the second set is for Evo-powered machines. If so, then H-D built 1,079 of the Shovelhead FXRS (versus 1,731 Evo) and 834 of the Shovelhead FXRT (versus 1,196 Evo) in 1984. In addition, a limited edition FXRDG and FXRSDG Disc Glides were built, and all are thought to be Evo-powered, but a few may have been assembled with the Evo motor.

Cross-Country Riding

From 1966 to the advent of the Honda Gold Wing, nothing existed other than the big Harleys when it came to cross-country touring. A lot of other bikes could be set up for long-distance riding by the addition of saddlebags, fairings, and the like. Some could haul two people in relative comfort, but none could equal the feeling of a big Harley. Motorcycling in this country always has been much more than a way to cover distance. Americans never have had to face extremely high gas prices and prohibitive taxes on engine size that most of the rest of the world has seen. In other countries, the motorcycle is a cheap necessary mode of transportation for a lot of families.

I was in China in the 1980s, and I got to learn a little about the people during a one-month vacation throughout the country along with seven other riders on large motorcycles. The amount of attention we garnered taught me what it must be like to be a movie star or political leader. People would gather around at every stop and just stare at us. My wife had long blond hair—very unknown in the Guangdong Province on the South China Sea. Women would come up to her and run their fingers across her hair to see if the color was painted on or real.

Bicycles are the main mode of transportation for millions upon millions of people. Riding a motorcycle is a real improvement in social status. It was not uncommon to see a father, his wife, two kids, and of course a cargo weighing over 50kg traveling down the streets of Shanghai on a 90cc bike. Sometimes even a pig or two got tucked in baskets tied to the front forks. Things are improving in China to the point where automakers will be introducing a 1300cc car in the near future, and more and more Toyotas and Nissans can be found fighting for space with the diesel taxis, but a family of four on a 125cc motorcycle will be very

For 1983, Harley came out with the FXRT Sport Glide. It was the FXR with a new frame-mounted fairing and hard saddlebags. The chain ran fully enclosed for extended life, and it had an anti-dive system incorporated in the front forks. The rear shocks had air assist. This bike was intended to compete with other sport tourers of the day from Europe and Japan. It met a lot of sales resistance from traditionalists but proved to be a good touring machine with a sporting bent. Good bike or no, it only lasted until 1987. *Harley-Davidson*

common for the foreseeable future.

In America, if we want to cover distances, we take a car. Nowhere else has cheap four-wheeled transportation been so readily available. Some sociologists state that the car was instrumental in freeing American youth and starting the migration from farms to urban life. Motorcycles have always been perceived as a statement, as opposed to necessary transportation, in this country. From the earliest board-track racing eighty years ago to the current retro bikes, Harley has been the maximum macho statement. Not many other types of hobbies are tattooed on peoples arms like Harley-Davidson. What's the possibility of a golf pro with "Tru-Flite" adorning a bicep?

People who ride Harleys, ride Harleys. If they could have a faster, smoother, cheaper bike, they'd still buy a Harley. A lot of people want the big bad image but use a Japanese cruiser to do it. The 20-year Harley owners would rather have an H-D in a box than a Honda Shadow in the garage. The past few years' reduced sales of Honda Gold Wings and Yamaha Ventures have left H-D virtually owning the big-bike market. Sales of BMW big bikes have increased tremendously, but the two manufacturers sell to different markets.

But people don't want a bike that's cantankerous, leaks, or breaks. The image of bikers with their cigarettes rolled up in T-shirt sleeves has given way to people of both sexes in designer clothes riding

Dave St. Onge is the sales manager for San Jose, Harley-Davidson in San Jose California. He started getting his hands greasy back in 1977 during the Shovelhead heyday. He worked everywhere from parts nugget up to service manager for two shops and was part owner of a Harley repair shop in Santa Cruz, California, for a number of years.

"When I first became interested in Harleys, 1977 and '78, they didn't have the screaming demand that they have enjoyed for the past decade. The new 1978 models came out in September and we hung through winter selling a few bikes to die-hard owners and other people with no better sense than to ride off on a new bike when the thermometer read below 30deg.

"Come the spring and we could be assured of a goodly stock of bikes sitting on the showroom floor. The rush to buy hit us around April 1, cleaning out 50 to 70 bikes in a hurry, but prior to spring, a potential customer had his pick of anything in just about any color. Our allotment never varied much from 80 bikes per year. The big shops, like Dudley Perkins, in San Francisco, usually saw anywhere from 150 to 175 per year; however, the smaller shops were pretty much in the same league as us.

"The way dealers qualified for bikes was, and is, kind of strange. If you're not in the new-vehicle business, you might not know that current year's allocations were based on the number of bikes sold the years before. Harley has a dealer's show once a year, around January, usually, where all the dealers from the U.S. and other countries get together for a few days of new-model introductions, renewing old acquaintances, spending money at the bar, and, most importantly, sitting down with the district rep and figuring out what bikes would be ordered for the following year.

"These days, it's pretty much take what you get, in the way of a standardized package—so many FLs, so many Dyna Glides, so many Sportys—all based on past sales performance. If the factory-can build a few extra bikes, you might get the option of picking up two or three more during the year, but that's all. Say the factory builds what they call a "Police Officer's Special," not a police bike, but a bike that they prefer be owned by a current or retired peace officer. It will have a different color combination, and that's about all. The dealership might get lucky and see three—all pre-sold.

"This isn't quite how it worked in the Shovelhead era. Sometimes, the next year's model bikes arrived in their crates while you were still trying to sell the current models sitting on the showroom floor. Just like everything else on earth, H-D responds to the law of supply and demand. New models sitting in your back room? Time to drop the price on the showroom units and move them out.

"Most of the dealers didn't own all their bikes, but purchased them through a "flooring" plan. Harley built the bikes and sent them to the dealers as they rolled off the assembly lines throughout the year. A finance company, like ITT Financial, actually owned the paper on the bikes and charged something in the neighborhood of one percent per month on the unpaid balance. The payback price to the flooring company sometimes dropped as the new model year approached. So a bike that had a sticker price of $6,995 in 1981 might have a flooring cost of $5,456 when it first hits your dealership. As the bike ages, you pay the flooring per month to keep it, making for a large motivation for the dealer to sell what's on the floor, rather than special order something almost identical to an existing bike.

"When the time nears for new-model intro, usually H-D would send you a modified flooring sheet. For instance, using the dealer cost figure of $5,456, after the bike has sat on the rug from November of the preceding year, H-D might send out a modified price of $5,195. This allowed you to reduce the price of your 1982 FXRS by $300 before the 1983 models came out, priced $250 higher. From 1978 to 1986, when the Evo really started taking off, it wasn't unusual at all to see 30 or more bikes sitting on the showroom floor, identical paint and options, only difference being model year. I saw times when two identical bikes, one year apart, sat on the floor, separated by $500.

"The Shovel usually could be counted on to return for at least two or three warranty problems. Sometimes in the late 1970s and early 1980s when AMF was pushing product out the door and letting the customer do the final engineering, it was not unusual to see an FXE return in 450mi with engine problems. At one point, I heard H-D was spending more money on bring-backs than they were making on the new bikes.

"Back when all the bikes came with kick-starters, most of the buyers were die-hard, bugs in the teeth, squashed 50-mission-cap-type riders; they were willing to put up with the Shovel's problems because everything on the road had problems. Triumphs had weird electrics, BSAs shook themselves to death, and Honda had just moved up from 250 and 305cc bikes to a big black 450 in 1966, but the Japanese weren't to be worried about, because all they knew was how to build little bikes. So an FLH vibrated—so what; they all vibrated. If you wanted smooth—take the train. You rode a motorcycle—particularly a Harley—you better be ready to put up with a little discomfort.

"Also, you better be able to put up with working on your bike all the time. A lot of early riders thought nothing of riding through the summer with nothing more than an oil change, a set of plugs, a flat tire, and maybe a clutch cable snapping, or pulling the chain and boiling it in oil (true!), and then putting the bike up in the winter months for a rebuild. Sometimes the rebuild went all the way down to splitting the cases, sometimes it was just a clean-up pass through the cylinders with a hone and a set of new rings, but it was always something.

"Things got better when H-D bought itself out. I saw a lot of the late-production Shovels—say early 1980s—come through my shop with high mileage on them, 40,000 wasn't unusual,

without ever having the heads off. Although when the country went to unleaded gas, it raised hell with the valves in the Shovels, as they relied on the lead to help lubricate the valve stem. Most of the Shovels on the road today have had the unleaded conversion, or the owner has resorted to some pretty trick things like aviation gas, aniline oil, or other additives to keep the valves from wearing prematurely.

"The last years of the Shovel, it actually quit going through oil so rapidly. Today an owner would hit the roof if an engine went through a quart of oil every 600mi (plus the EPA wouldn't let the vehicle be sold). In 1966, it wasn't unusual to "lose" a quart every 450–500mi. Even in 1979, getting 670mi to a quart was considered OK.

"In 1981, an oil-control package cleaned up the bikes considerably. Better seals, closer tolerances, and an oil-return line from the heads help double oil mileage.

"Today, not many Shovelheads come through the dealership. After all, it's been 11 years since the last one went out a dealer's door. The ones we do see run in two very distinct categories. Either they are as close to stock and perfect as the owners and their wallets can make them, or they are on their sixth through fifteenth owners and look like they have been thoroughly used and abused. Luckily some owners have caught on to the fact that a Harley doesn't get worth less as it ages, so long as it is kept in reasonable shape. A good Shovel might not make you money, but it's the only bike that you can ride and enjoy for 10 years and still sell it for at least what you paid.

"In some cases, you will actually make money if you sit on the bike for a while. I just wish I had the money to buy some of the bikes that rolled through the shop over the past 15 years. There was actually times when a 1970s Shovel could be picked up for less than $4,000 with under 5,000mi on the clock. What do they call that—20-20 hindsight?"

The Harley Owner's Group

At about the same time H-D filed for the tariff against its Japanese competitors, it also instituted a number of programs aimed at improving their product and changing the company's image from outlaw bikers to wholesome sport riders. One of the greatest ideas to bring customers closer to the company was the formation of the Harley Owner's Group (HOG). More mileage has been made with the use of this one word than any other in H-D's inventory of trademarked logos.

If you are a member of HOG, you know what's available through the largest factory supported club in the world. If you aren't a member, join. My last *Hog Tales*, the club magazine, has more rallies and events going on than you could attend if you had twice as much money and only worked half the year. This year, alone, there are events in places like Australia, where the sixth annual Australian HOG rally is taking place in Queensland, to the fifth annual European rally in Spain. These rallies and the ones in the United States have become so popular that they are usually sold out well in advance and crowds can easily run to 50,000.

Also, if you want a chance to ride a particular model without having to buy it first, HOG holds demo rides all around the States, usually tied in with bike shows or races. A riding schedule can be found in their magazine. Be prepared for lots of people, though. The Laughlin Run, in Laughlin, Nevada, has grown to such a size that all hotel rooms and campsites are reserved at least six months in advance. The town, situated on the Colorado River where it splits Arizona and Nevada, turns into a motorcycle town for the three days of the run. For almost a week on either side of the run dates, motorcycles fill the surrounding areas to capacity. Last I heard, 1995 saw 55,000 people attending.

---

reliable, clean bikes. No one wants to have to heave on a kickstarter for 5min on a warm day in order to ride a bike. If the Shovelhead, with all its amenities, hadn't come along and paved the way for even better scooters, H-D might still be selling 6,000 FLHs per year to the same group of die-hard riders. In a very major way, the Shovelhead was instrumental in opening the sport of touring and big bikes to the world. Bikes had to change if motorcycling was to become widely accepted as a recreational sport.

People wanted an image, but they weren't willing to put up with what it took in the past to maintain that image. The old one-percenters (the one percent of riders who created 99 percent of the problems) became a thing of the past. We've been able to beat down the image of a big, dirty dude on a Harley scaring unmitigated hell out of citizens and causing daughters to be locked inside when he rolls into town.

The movie *The Wild One*, released in December 1953 and starring Marlon Brando and an actor, relatively unknown at the time, named Lee Marvin created an image that took decades to live down. Brando actually rode a Triumph throughout the whole movie—never a Harley. Lee Marvin and his boys rode the Harleys. Most of the cycle scenes were at the beginning of the movie. The balance of it was Brando wandering around in confusion trying to find himself. The movie was banned in England for years because of the image it portrayed.

The Wild One was somewhat based in fact. A gang, known as "The Booze Fighters," not the Hells Angels, rode into a sleepy Northern California town, Hollister, back on July 4, 1947, got drunk, fell off bikes, rode on the sidewalk, fell down some more, got their picture in *Life* magazine, and generally scared the hell out of the locals. No one died, got raped, got shot, or anything major, but it did set a precedent for years to come.

In the 1960s, I rode over a lot of the West Coast on my Panhead. After riding it stock for a few years, I changed over to the long-forks-and-black-paint chopper look. One day riding into Virginia City, Nevada, I was met by two shotgun-toting sheriffs at the city limits who told me I wasn't welcome in their town. I couldn't even ride through. I had to turn around and go back "where your kind of trash belongs." This was just

me, nobody else; I had left all my napalm and machine guns at home, opting for a tent and sleeping bag instead. I had said exactly zero to the cops when they stopped me. I had short hair, a helmet, and was sober as a judge (wrong simile?); they just didn't like motorcycles, especially big, black Harley motorcycles. Perhaps if I'd been riding a Honda 250, painted light yellow, they wouldn't have been so scared of me.

Point being, we've come a long way on bikes, and it took a good one like the Shovelhead to begin the process.

The FXRS didn't change much in 1983. It still was the best-handling bike produced by Harley. Sales for the FXRS dropped to 1,413; the FXR sold 1,129. The rubber-mounted engine, high-speed handling capabilities, and superb brakes helped it keep up with the canyon runners, but buyers that wanted the Low Rider look and function came a distant second. *Harley-Davidson*

Index